Praise for *Brother Com*

This very personal and honest
tion of her feelings as she exper...
welcome news that she has an older brother. That excitement, though, is somewhat tempered by his very existence being a long-held secret and one that will not readily be revealed to any but immediate family. Her elation at having "found" an older brother takes no account of the impact this event has on either her mother or her father.

Her account of the joy she experiences in the ensuing years as she gets to know her brother is moderated by him remaining a "secret". Peppered throughout this story about both her brother and her mother, one senses regret at conversations that didn't happen and questions that were never answered. It's a reminder that life is not infinite and that we must cherish the time we have with those we love and ensure the questions we seek answers to have been posed and explored.

Throughout the narrative we gain an impression of Ross as a larger-than-life personality, likeable and charismatic, who was professionally very capable and successful but a man whose personal life was at times chaotic and at odds with his public success. Lynne is left with unanswered questions about the rather complex but full life her brother led.

Regardless, one is left with the certainty that despite everything, Lynne loved both her brother and her mother wholeheartedly.

I highly recommend reading this poignant and at times amusing book. It will both move you and stimulate reflection about the relationships that are important to you, the reader.

MARILYN WELSH, holder of senior management roles in governmental and not-for-profit organizations. Ross's first wife and mother of their children, Emma and James.

Brother Come, Brother Go is a book that will stay with you long after you turn the final page. It's a testament to the enduring power of family, the healing power of truth, and the transformative beauty of shared experiences. Whether you have a sibling yourself or simply navigate the intricate web of family relationships, this book offers laughter, tears, and a profound sense of connection.

With unflinching honesty and aching love, the author delves into the tangled web of secrets, sacrifices, and unspoken truths that bind siblings together. I laughed, I cried, and most importantly, I recognized myself—my own joys, vulnerabilities, and the complexities that weave through every family's tapestry.

This book isn't just a story; it's an invitation to explore your own history. Thought-provoking questions at the end of each section guide you inward, sparking "ah-ha" moments and challenging your comfortable narratives. These questions act as gentle nudges, reflecting your own story back at you, inviting introspection and self-discovery.

The author's talent lies in her ability to paint vivid portraits of characters, their joys and sorrows, their strengths and vulnerabilities, mirroring the people we know and love. You'll find yourself nodding in recognition, chuckling at familiar quirks, and blinking back tears at moments of profound vulnerability.

So, dive into this compelling narrative. Let the author's voice become your guide, and prepare to be touched, challenged, and ultimately, transformed by the echoes of family secrets and the universal language of shared humanity.

JENNIFER SANDERS, Coach and Consultant

Also by Lynne Burney

Once a Pilgrim, Always a Coach

Brother Come, Brother Go

27/7/24

Dear Tina

Thank you for listening. Now do the reading! I hope my story connects with yours.

Best wishes

Lynne x

BROTHER COME, BROTHER GO

A story of three birthdays,
two funerals, and a wedding

LYNNE BURNEY

LKB PUBLISHING
PARIS, FRANCE

LKB Publishing
Paris, France
Copyright © 2024 by Lynne Burney. All rights reserved.
Cataloging-in-Publication Data is on file with the Library of Congress
Paperback ISBN: 978-2-9584245-3-4
eBook ISBN: 978-2-9584245-4-1

Book design by Christina Thiele

www.lkb-coaching.com

To my brother, Ross
Met so late—left too soon
To my mother, Maureen
No one gets this mother business right the first time.
To my father, Brian
I only remember the good times.
To my sister, Maxine, a painter of life's journeys
You're there when it counts.
To my son, Christophe
Everyone and everything, belongs.

Contents

Preface	xiii
Foreword	xv

PART ONE
Happy Birthday—July 21st, 1994 — 1

PART TWO
And the Beat Goes On—The Interim years — 43

PART THREE
Party's Over—The WhatsApp Dialogues, 2021 — 95

PART FOUR
It's No Picnic—January 2023 — 141

PART FIVE
It's a Long Way Home — 163

PART SIX
Denudare—To Uncover — 215

Acknowledgements — 227
About the Author — 229

Author's Preface

As with all life, there is a beginning and an end. What happens in between is the stuff of stories. Some tales beg to be told and others are more reticent; they wait patiently for their storyteller to come along. When she does, she takes each event and decks it in a cloth and colour of her own making and tells it in a way that convinces you that she is telling the truth. That is the stuff of a good story.

This story was originally called "Ordinary Traumas," based on the origin of the word in Greek, meaning "wound." Life wounds and who could say, in all honesty, that life has not been wounding in some way? But to use the word "ordinary" to describe trauma might diminish the sense of damage done to many people who have experienced traumatic events. It could well have been called "Family Secrets." They do indeed wreak havoc on a family system but they do not pre-suppose trauma. Finally, its title is *"Brother Come, Brother Go."* It is light in tone, mirroring the expression "Easy come—easy go." It's a bit about trauma, a bit about secrets, a lot about love and loss and mostly about the life of an ordinary family. The characters laugh and love and grieve. The wounds sometimes gape and ooze. The Band-Aids don't always stick and the doctor doesn't come in time. It's called Life and it comes and it goes.

Above all, it is my story.

Foreword

In the preface to her book *Brother Come, Brother Go*, Lynne writes, "each storyteller decks events in cloth and colours of her own making and tells it in a way that convinces you she is telling the truth."

So, is she telling the truth?

Her title and her wink to storytelling and truth invite me into the fields of therapy and Buddhism, both of which I am deeply involved in professionally and personally. This is what I find.

It is a story in which a specific unique experience, that of Lynne and her New Zealand family, crosses paths with the universal journey of our shared human emotional experience of life and death.

As Lynne mentions in her preface, the book title was originally "Ordinary Traumas" and, given my professional background as a therapist, I am deeply sensitive to the way in which awareness of trauma has exploded into the world of mental health, counselling, and therapy since Dr Bessel van der Koch redefined trauma as relational. His breakthrough work has opened the concept for common usage of the term "trauma."

Yes, the origin of the word is from the Greek meaning "wound" as Lynne points out. Yes, "the wounds sometimes gape and ooze, the Band-Aids don't always stick and the doctor doesn't come in time." I agree with Lynne when she writes, "It's called Life and it comes and it goes."

So why read this story? What can we learn from Lynne's unique experience that is relevant to all of us? What can we learn about dealing with the "stuff" of Life? I am helped by Mark Epstein's skillful description of the Buddha's experience of Awakening over 2,500 years ago. It is a guideline for facing life and its everyday potential for trauma. I am struck by the way Lynne's own story reminds me once again of the ways to move from suffering to the end of suffering. Lynne's book offers the reader an example of a passageway through pain and suffering. As a therapist and Buddhist, it is an opportune moment to reconsider the traditional definition of trauma and revisit the lessons of the Buddha. What is this new thinking? What are these old lessons?

1. Trauma is a fact of life, not a failure or a mistake. Face it.
2. The way forward is the way through.
3. Self-Awareness guides us.
4. There is a Relational Home for all our feelings.

Lesson 1: Face what is.

To quote Mark Epstein from his book *Everyday Trauma*:

"If one can treat trauma as a fact, not as a failure, one has a chance to learn from the inevitable slings and arrows that come one's way.... the traumas of everyday life, if they do not destroy us, become bearable, even illuminating, when we learn to relate to them differently."

We find this lesson being learnt by Lynne in her New Zealand family. Even when some members of her family choose the way of denial and dissociation from life's inevitable pain, we see her honest attempt to face what can shock and wound her and to relate to it differently from her inherited cultural reactions.

This can help us to reflect on our own attitudes to the fact of impermanence. Are we using the same attitudes handed down to us through the culture we were born into? Are we seeing differently from other members of our family? What secrets are there in our family archives?

Lynne's first theme is secrets: Her story starts with a family secret being revealed. She refuses to become entangled in questions about a past her parents have created; instead, she takes a different path.

"I know from my work that shame and blame are killers. When I look at my brother, I cannot see my mother's shame and I do not know who blames whom for what. Does Mum blame Dad for his years of silence? Does Dad blame Mum because she gave away his son without consulting him? Is this true? I don't know.

On this first day of his life in our family these subterranean thoughts do not surface to become a conversation. We do not talk about the whys and what ifs; we celebrate the NOW!"

Could we have done that? To have chosen the now, where joy could be embraced? Thank you, Lynne, for this lesson that when we face a situation head-on, we meet the Eternal Now, where all is potential. We have a choice.

Lesson 2: The way forward is the way through.

Lynne's story could have stopped at a happy ending, but instead it goes onto the wound of loss. What gets her through seems to be the compelling story of her feelings as she accompanies those closest to her towards their deaths.

Lesson 3: Self -Awareness is our guide.

Trauma, we now know, is not caused by traumatic events but by the way we relate to them. How will Lynne experience these inevitable losses? What can we learn from her? Can we let ourselves explore the fullness of our losses without losing our point of reference, our self-awareness? For this is what Lynne does in her story.

Lesson 4: There is a Relational Home for all our feelings.

The story of Lynne's feelings for her brother, her father and her mother and for the New Zealand that held them all in its cultural patterns, is a story of inclusion. We are introduced to their world, their inheritance. The richness of Ross in his passions and achievements in his community are a story in themselves. Her feelings for her father are simple: she took what he had shared with thanks, whereas her feelings towards her mother emerge in all their complexity. No hiding from the hurt, the disappointments, the anger, as well as the emergence of deep love and acceptance.

So here we have the story of how Lynne finds a home for her feelings, showing us the resilience we humans can create by the way we relate to each other and to our everyday traumas. Traumas can become bearable and even illuminating. We find ourselves in our stories. Try this story—it may lead you to yours!

Jennifer de Gandt

Coaching elder and therapist—pioneer of Neuro Linguistic programming and CLEAN Coaching in France

PART ONE

Happy Birthday

NEW ZEALAND
JULY 21ST, 1994 (THURSDAY NIGHT)

"We have something to tell you," my father said. I know what's coming. I adjust my sitting position at the table: straighten my back and place my feet, slightly apart, flat on the floor. I am ready to receive the news that, after all these years of discontent, they are finally going to separate.

"What would you say if you knew you had a brother?"

It is ten o'clock on a cold winter night in New Zealand. The question spins down the table and freezes in the space between the end of the main course and the birthday cake. I do not move. I'm aware that I'm sitting opposite my mother, that my sister is to my left and my father, to my right. My ten-year-old son has left the table. My father has tossed his curveball from his usual place at the head of the table; his casual tone suggests he could be asking for a second helping of roast.

My father belongs to a generation of New Zealand men who say little of any consequence in the company of women. I don't know if these men have nothing to say or just clam up in the presence of women. I don't recall ever having been invited beyond the barrier of social banter with my dad, so don't have any clue as to what he is thinking right now. I'm in a state of animated suspension.

My dad, however, has a capacity for calm when shit hits the fan. It might be a throw over from his days in the navy. I don't know for sure, but I did witness it several times while growing up.

I remember, when I was fifteen, going to a party and drinking apple cider thinking it was fizzy apple juice. My escort poured me through the front door of our house in the early hours of the following morning, legless drunk. Dad sat me down on the bed, made me a cup of hot chocolate and murmured sympathetically that I was in for "one hell of a head." Mum, on the other hand, lashed me with words meant to shame and punish. She was screaming her worry, but I was too young and too sozzled to hear her love for me behind the fear.

Now, sitting around the table, celebrating my forty-second birthday with my family in Napier, I give no thought to her fears and, least of all, her love.

As if Dad's question were her cue, my mother stands up and begins collecting up our plates and scraping the leftovers onto the top plate. She carefully arranges the dirty knives and forks on top of the scraps.

"It ruined our marriage," she mumbles, blushing before turning her back on the table.

"It hurt me too," my father adds quietly in a rare moment of expressed personal truth. It contradicts all my previous experience of him. I can't process his statement right now, but I don't hear it as an accusation.

Somehow my sister, six years my junior, knows this brother is first and that I have lost rank. She gasps in unadorned delight. "Ha! You're not the first!"

My mind is wildly scrambling through unassembled data; scraps of information tumbling through layers of time. It's as if I am watching jigsaw pieces whirling around in space. Suddenly, they click together. I see a poker machine in a games arcade. A row of identical fruit line up and the machine flashes, "JACKPOT!" Coins are gushing through its narrow metal mouth. Their clatter shakes me to ask, "When are we going to meet him?"

"Tomorrow. He's arriving for the weekend." A simple response from my father.

His first ten-tonne curveball has already exploded the hitherto calm lake this family gathering was floating on, but his second curveball launches a tsunami. In the aftermath, my sister and I gain a brother; my son, an uncle; and my parents, a son. The only wreckage is a family secret.

"Why didn't you tell us we had a brother?" my sister asks, slightly indignant.

"I would have gone to the grave without telling you, but he called me." Mum says as if answering a prosecutor.

"How old is he?" I ask, ignoring my mother's monstrously honest statement.

"Forty-three."

My brain is throbbing numbers and questions: I was born in July and am forty-two. He is forty-three. What month was he born in? Technically, how is that possible? Where was he born? No thought as to what Mum and Dad might be feeling now the cat is out of the bag interferes with my feverish calculations. I am impervious to how it feels to release a secret kept for forty-three years into the universe; how it will take shape and size and colour and belong to the world; how it can never be taken back into the silent arms of an expectant mother; how the landscape of all our worlds just changed, permanently. None of this is in the forefront of my mind right now.

Only "What's his name?" No visible turmoil.

"Ross," she replies. No visible emotion.

How lovely, I think. I turn his name around in my head, not quite trusting to say it out loud yet. I hear the short, sharpness of the single syllable, *Ross*.

I have a brother called Ross, I say again to myself. *I have a brother called Ross who is older than me and he's coming for the weekend*, I repeat to myself, willing myself to stay calm, in control, up to the situation—as always—as expected.

In my sister's initial thrill of realizing that I am not her perfect older sister, but second in line, she begins to wildly speculate about what she could give our brother as a welcome home gift. I'm only half listening to her even though I'm smiling and making encouraging nods in her direction.

I'm trolling through time, searching for any clues that pointed to Ross's existence. A memory pushes its nose to the surface. I am standing with my mother beside the linen cupboard, in the hallway of our three-bedroomed home at 20 Achilles Street, Christchurch. I must be around eleven or twelve. We are talking birthdays. I remember that she gets the year of my birth wrong. She is out by a year. I leap with glee on the discrepancy and show off my newfound knowledge of an adult word. "You mean I'm a bastard!" I say, showing her I know that if you are born before your parents are married, that makes you a bastard. "You said I was born in 1951, but you and Dad were married in 1952." I have no doubt about my own legitimacy, so I'm surprised that she is not as delighted as I am with my budding sophistication.

We both know I was born in July 1952. Her face goes a deep shade of red and she corrects her error in a flustered voice. She is clearly annoyed and does not appreciate my choice of words.

It is strange how that memory has stayed with me for over thirty years and comes back with great clarity now. I knew without knowing that someone was missing.

I wonder if Maxine, too, has a memory similar to mine. Much later in life she does confirm that she also remembered a time when she announced at the dinner table in Napier, when she was at high school and I was no longer living at home, that she wished she had an older brother. She remembered that there was nowhere to go with the conversation after that.

We both knew, without knowing, someone was missing in our lives.

I pull my mind back to the dinner table in July 1994, to the aftermath of the tsunami and tune into my sister's excitement. It's catching and I quickly join her in trying to imagine what kind of person we will be meeting tomorrow evening. I am also silently focusing on what to wear. It's like a blind date: not too sexy—first date; not too classic—boring; not too fancy—trying too hard; not too casual—uncaring.... What do I wear to greet a forty-three-year-old brother I have never met? What kind of gift could make him feel welcome after such a long absence?

My sister and I stay at the table. Mum continues to move dishes around and goes back and forth to the kitchen, not saying anything. Dad remains at his place at the head of the table and is following our conversation. While my sister and I are talking welcome presents, I am wondering what our parents are feeling about their son coming to meet their daughters.

It's all too stark for me.

"I had been expecting his call for forty-three years," she adds.

How is it even possible to wait forty-three years for your child to call you? What kind of welcome gift could possibly make up for forty-three years of silence?

But I am excited too. How many people get a brother for their forty-second birthday? I have something I can share with my sister. We've never shared anything before, other than our common parentage. I hardly know her at all. We have rarely been in the same town, let alone the same country, at the same time, to share any kind of family event.

What to buy Ross? Our ideas bubble and fizz like a freshly opened bottle of champagne until well after midnight. Maxine is going to embroider a cushion with

Indian elephants. I am thinking that a men's perfume is a safer bet. Neither of us mentions the oddness of the event that we are planning for. We seem to have a tacit agreement that we don't talk about "it" in the house.

JULY 22ND (FRIDAY MORNING)

Mum and Dad no longer live on the hill that dominates the town of Napier. The hill was thrown up in the 1931 earthquake. The 7.8 quake levelled most of the buildings downtown, killed over 200 people, and injured many more. The town, with its "new" hill, was rebuilt in the 1930s in the style of the time: Art Deco. It's now recognised as the world capital of this type of architecture and design.

Mum and Dad left their house on the hill when their multilevel garden became too much to manage as they grew older. They invested in a house on the flat with a swimming pool when two salaries allowed them to enjoy the luxury. When they retired, they opted for a more compact house with three bedrooms and less luxurious add-ons.

It's around ten the following morning when we finally set out from the house on our quest for a greet-the-brother gift. My son stays home with his grandparents. The sky is a sharp winter blue. A July sun is teasing us with promises of warmth that fools neither fingertips nor nose. We are both dressed to resist the crisp air currents coming in from the sea and the shady corners downtown where the sun's rays don't reach. Within thirty minutes we are peering into shop windows in the centre of the town.

It's strange to be walking alongside my sister and chatting away to her. We were separated when I was sixteen and she was ten, by the simple act of our parents moving to a different town from the one we had grown up in. They left me to finish my schooling and took her with them so she could continue hers. Lifestyle change. Exciting for a sixteen-year-old. I don't know how it was for her and I'm not going to ask her now. We have a mission.

My sister knows this town well, having done her high school education locally. I got married in the public gardens here, just across the road from Mum and Dad's house on the hill, but I couldn't say I know the town the way she does. I know next to nothing about her life and imagine she knows little of mine. I think things will change with a brother to share. She doesn't wear a wedding ring and I have taken mine off. I removed it when I left my son's father a year prior to this trip. I had bought our two silver wedding bands from one of the shops here in 1980. Fourteen years later I doubt I will find the jewellery store again. At some point in the future, I will wonder if there is any connection between leaving a husband and finding a brother. It's no more than a flirt with consciousness this fine winter morning.

I am happy to let my sister be my shopping guide. We amble along the sidewalk of the main street chatting about what sort of thing would be appropriate to give our new brother. Maxine has an eye for intricate detail. She likes the swirling vibrant and brilliantly coloured lines of Indian designs. I like the simple, stark, straight lines of Swedish designs. From her point of view my tastes probably lack warmth and comfort; hers are too cluttered and fussy for me. It's not certain that we will find something that we can both agree on. While we are asking ourselves questions about this brother we have just been given, we are not having to choose anything so there is no chance of disagreement. I feel like I am meeting my sister as well as my brother. In the space of an evening, I have been pushed from the mentality of an only child to finding myself in the middle—between a brother and a sister. The feeling is akin to a hit on a joint that introduces a surrealistic element to reality. I'm conscious of the sharpness of the air and the bold outlines of the shop windows and sidewalks. I'm on a movie set and the cameras are rolling. It's not a bad feeling.

We eventually wander into a store that sells all

kinds of odds and ends. Nothing is secondhand, but the choice is so vast that we know instantly that we've found the right shop, if not the actual item yet. I pick up bookends: too heavy; he's flying. I read out a few titles of books on display: too risky; does he even like reading? Maxine flicks through a rack of bathrobes: too personal; we know nothing about him, except that he has two kids and a second wife. I hold up a beer mug with "Ross" written on it: too cheap; besides, maybe he only drinks wine. We continue wandering around the store, holding up items, discussing the pros and cons of each, eventually deciding against and moving on to the next potential gift. The shop assistant looks bored and seems happy to let us get on with our "mission impossible" without her help.

I don't know who sees him first. He is tucked away behind some Tibetan bowls. He is carved in white wood. His ears are long, his eyebrows are arched, his eyes are downcast, the corners of his mouth are slightly raised in a hint of a smile, his shoulders are squared, the fingers of his right hand are very long and a wooden lotus is poised between the tips of his index and middle fingers and thumb. He is seated in the lotus position and he is about twenty centimetres in height. He's the one!

We find out that he has been made in Indonesia. He is not a Buddha. He is a wiseman, sitting peacefully with himself and his lotus. He is a little rough around the edges but perfectly balanced. He is wrapped up for us; we share the cost. He is easy to hold; we carry him out of the shop and make our way home.

JULY 22ND (FRIDAY NIGHT)

The afternoon disappears without note. The sun is down by five o'clock. We are all sitting in the lounge, waiting. My son and only child knows something really big is going on, but I don't know how well we have explained it to him. He's sitting between his aunt and me on the couch. Mum and Dad are seated in armchairs on either side of the room. They are silent. I have stage fright. My sister babbles. My son is just watching us.

The doorbell rings. We all stand in one simultaneous solemn movement. Dad takes five assertive strides to the front door and opens it with gusto. He proffers his right hand in a manly fashion and says in a hearty voice, "Come in—we've been waiting for you!" He shakes his son's hand vigorously. I catch the beam on his face.

Ross—son—brother—uncle bursts through the doorway, arms out wide, a smile the size of a bus stop.

"Gidday! How are y'—I'm Ross."

JULY 23ᴿᴰ (SATURDAY MORNING)

The toast is still warm and sitting expectantly in its rack on the table laid with silver cutlery and my mother's best dishes. There is a choice of cereals in three different glass bowls. The milk has been poured into a matching glass jug. These are arranged on a tablecloth of pale gold swirls printed on high-quality, sea-green cotton. Each has its place and each seems ready to put its best foot forward. Six places have been laid. The kettle is on the boil.

We all enter centre stage from the hallway at about the same time and take our places, ready for a repeat performance of last night's "normality" show. I am loving every minute of my role in our very own family pageant. I am "Sis." I have never been a "Sis" before. Everything is on offer: sugar, milk, coffee, tea, toast, jams, honey, and vegemite.

We tuck in with enthusiasm. We banter, chat, laugh, and generally keep the conversation on high octane. Well, Maxine, Ross, and I do. Mum doesn't really sit down to breakfast. She fusses around, filling cups, checking on toast, milk, jam. Dad just listens, a charmed and fixed smile on his face. My son tries to keep up as far as his ten years will allow him. The closest we get to the risqué is when my sister lays it on with an impersonation of a Bacall-Bogart big-screen dialogue, "So, where've y' been all our lives, Bro?"

To which he replies in the same tone, "Jus' waitin' f' you guys t' come along."

The conversation lulls.

We giggle—a bit too enthusiastically.

Ross tells us about putting the call through to "Mother" after he had buried "Dad." I am feeling confused about who's who, but he's my brother and he can have as many mothers and fathers as he likes.

I absolutely do not know who he is, but I like him enormously. I love his smile, his laughter, the deep tones of his voice and the way he articulates his words. I like his dark-rimmed glasses, the white shirt he was wearing last night, the jeans he is wearing this morning. I like that he has come to the breakfast table freshly shaved and smelling of cologne. I like his short, sharp haircut; his hair that is just starting to turn grey, his receding hairline. I like that he is just slightly taller than me if he stands up straight. I like that I am thinner than him—he has a wee paunch that says he is an over-forty male. I liked his hug last night; I liked it again this morning. I like that he liked our gift of the wooden wiseman holding the roughly hewn lotus between his fingertips. It will go next to his piano, which I learn he knows how to play.

I remember one Christmas morning when I was

eight years old, waking to find the pillowcase I had left at the foot of my bed the night before stuffed full of presents. Father Christmas hadn't always been so generous, even though I was unwavering in the quantity of milk and cake I left out for him. I remember how I relished opening each one of those brightly wrapped parcels.

It's like that now. It's a bumper Christmas and I'm relishing every detail that Ross reveals of his life without us in it.

Ross goes on with the story about "the call" he put through to "Mother" one night, six months earlier.

"I asked a good mate of mine at Radio NZ to sit with me while I called the registry office in Wellington using my birth certificate. My dad gave it to me on his eightieth birthday. He told me to do with it what I thought was best. I had his blessing."

He is saying without saying that his adoption was never a secret—that he had always known.

Says who? I don't voice the irony.

"I spoke to a very nice woman who located Mother's number."

He calls Mum, "Mother," I note mentally but don't query.

"They located her address in Napier and had her phone number in hand in under ten minutes."

You can be lost for forty-three years and be found

in under ten minutes. I am incredulous but continue munching my muesli.

"It was early evening and there was only me and my mate left in the office. The woman asked me if I wanted her to make the call. I said I did. She asked if I was ready to either have my call accepted, or rejected. I said I was."

The Parable of the Prodigal Son flits across my mind. I remember it was the father who was overjoyed and had laid the table for a feast. In this case Mum has laid the feast but her joy over the return is not in evidence.

"So, she put through the call. I can still hear her asking Mother if she would be willing to accept a call from a Ross McRobie."

Mum cuts in at this point to say, "I said 'yes.' I had been expecting that call for forty-three years."

It is the second time in the last two days that I hear her say this. My ears pick up the whispering silence that weaves like a cat between the words "expecting" and "forty-three." I am so enamoured of my new brother that I give no thought to my mother's feelings. I am centred entirely on my own joy, fascination, curiosity. She is, in fact, forgotten, in this drive to make up for lost time, to close the gap, to be one big happy family. I am not sure who is driving fastest, my sister or myself. Or maybe it's Ross. Maybe he wants to feel included—be part of the family. I don't know.

Mum adds, "I recognised his first name. I gave it to him."

Another lull in the conversation.

Ross then says, "I grew up in Invercargill in the far south of the country, where I was born."

This is not news to Mum, but I look to her to explain how we got to Christchurch, where Maxine and I were born.

She says, simply, "After his birth, I went up to Auckland, got a job, and married your father when he came out of the navy. We went to Christchurch while I was expecting you."

So, she went from the far south to the far north and back to the middle again to start her married life as a mother. There is judgement in my calculation, but it is not spoken. I do not include my father in the equation. He is catalogued as an accessory, not as a protagonist. This is an incorrect assessment. He is indeed my brother's father as much as Mum is his true mother. Ross was indeed born out of wedlock while Dad was away in the navy. It is enough to look at them side by side to see the resemblance. Right now, however, Dad is even less in the forefront of my mind than my mother is. Anger will surface later and will not know where to put itself. But not now. Now is perfect.

"Mum and Dad were in their forties and childless when they adopted me," Ross continues candidly.

I beam. He was joy and loss in one tiny bundle. The paradox remains unacknowledged on this day, July 23rd, 1994, but it nevertheless continues to percolate just beneath the smooth appearance of things.

"Mum gave up work to take care of me," Ross carries on with his family story. It seems to flow from him like water off a duck's back. I can pretend to be a duck. Maybe he is pretending too. I don't know. I do know that our—my mum (I don't know which possessive adjective to use)—used to be an usherette in a city cinema theatre when I was little. I remember going to see *Batman* and *The Wizard of Oz* on a big screen for free on a Saturday afternoon. I remember how excited and terrified I was. I wonder if his "Mum" took him to see *Batman* on the big screen. Things I don't know and suddenly want to know because I have a brother who has just appeared in my life.

She would have gone to the grave without telling us, she had said on Thursday night.

What made her change her mind? I wonder. Then I remember: He called them. Why did he do that? He seems to read my mind because he says, "Mum and Dad died a few years apart and when Dad went, I just felt that it was time to try contacting my birth mother. I didn't know anything about you guys."

He means Maxine and I. No mention of Dad, I note.

I feel like I am operating outside the sphere of the known universe.

I had a boyfriend, Dick, when I was teaching at a high school in the Hutt Valley in 1975. He was adopted. I remember him screaming in anguish after a few too many wines, that his mother had wanted to flush him down the loo. I don't know how he knew that and I never knew the circumstances of his adoption. I don't remember the details of his story but I do remember how his pain surfaced and crashed all over the furniture in my upstairs flat.

What Ross is telling us over breakfast twenty years later doesn't match with my only other experience with someone who had been adopted. Dick was my boyfriend, not my brother. I have a sudden horrifying thought: *What if Ross and I had met and we had gone out together?* I almost gasp out loud at the thought. I really like him. Dating him would have been a possibility. What if all my dates had been unconscious stand-ins for my brother?

Except that I married a Frenchman—and the mere thought of an incestuous, albeit inadvertent, relationship with my brother is terrifying.

I look at my son with all his lovely, boyish energy. I

love him dearly. I loved him from the moment I saw him. I am struck, suddenly, by an awareness of my hitherto ignorance of the pain my mother must have carried in silence and resentment for forty-three years. What is it like for a woman who lets go of the child she has just given birth to? I have no access to the loneliness that women like her must feel, carrying the memory of rejection: theirs and their child's. I don't know the size, shape, or colour of this kind of loss.

"I have two kids: James and Emma," Ross says, tuning into my train of thought.

My son has two cousins about the same age as him. The story just gets better by the minute. I look at my son. He has to see them to believe them at his age. They are not real yet.

I'm still not ready to get up from the breakfast table, gripped as I am by a desire to hear the complete story of my brother's forty-three years, but am also aware that my son is getting restless and that Mum and Dad probably need a break from the intensity. It is a bright, sunny, winter's day outside but not much of it is in evidence; Dad has closed the venetian blinds. He has muttered something about what we do being nobody else's business. I realize with a blinding flash of pure fury that he is keeping the neighbours' eyes out—and the secret in. In that split second, I feel I am being consumed by a conflagration of unmitigated rage. There are no words.

"Let's clear up and get going!" Maxine, impatient, moves us on to the next part of the day and saves me from a meltdown.

JULY 23RD (SATURDAY AFTERNOON)

The morning has slid away. Lunch is over. The dishes are done. I don't remember a time when it was so much fun to wash and dry dishes. We are all intent on playing "happy families" and we really do make it happen. Now it's time for the "kids" to go out to play. Ross is forty-three, I am newly forty-two, and Maxine is thirty-six, but we are off to play together.

We rent a bicycle down on the waterfront for the real kid, my son, to ride. He's not very sure of himself on two wheels, but the Bro'—he is now my bro'—holds on to the back and runs along behind him shouting, "Great! You can do it! You're doing it! Go!"

Christophe is wearing his crash helmet; his head is down; his legs pump furiously. He has no awareness of the moment that Ross lets go. My son is riding a bicycle, on his own, just like all Kiwi kids his age. I am so happy—so proud. Christophe looks around and realizes it's just him and the bike. His pedalling becomes less assertive—he wobbles—he looks like he might fall. The Bro' and

I get ready to run after him. We both see him make a decision: he grips the handlebars, fixes the road ahead, pushes into the pedal, one after the other and he's on his way again. He can ride a bike!

My bro' has been in the family for less than a day and he has taught my son to ride a bicycle. This is what uncles and brothers and fathers are for.

On that very first day together I witness how much positive energy exudes from the pores of my brother's skin. As time goes on, I will see how that draws people towards him like the proverbial iron filings on a magnet. I am elated—laughing and clapping and shouting. Bursting with joy.

From my work as a coach, constellator of family and company systems and a very long yoga practice, I know that shame and blame are killers. When I look at my brother, I cannot see my mother's shame and do not know who blames whom for what. Does Mum blame Dad for his years of silence? Does Dad blame Mum because she gave away his son without consulting him? Is this true? I don't know.

On this first day of his life in our family, these subterranean thoughts do not surface to become a conversation. We do not talk about whys and what-ifs.

We celebrate the NOW!

JULY 23ʳᴅ (SATURDAY NIGHT)

Tea is a quick affair of leftovers from lunch. We seem to have exhausted all we are willing and able to share of our respective lives for one day. I don't know who suggests that we go to a pub, but the idea is met with enthusiasm. The three of us set off together around 8pm, leaving grandparents and grandson to Saturday night TV and hot chocolate.

The night air is chilly, the moon is almost full, and it's hard to say if the bounce in our step is to keep warm or a simple expression of shared joy. We are happy. Who could possibly understand, most of all the husband I have recently left, or the man I have left him for, that this brother IS the man I have been unconsciously seeking in all my relationships? He is the empty space I have sensed and sought to fill all my life. That this gap has been explained—and in such a joyful way—brings profound relief to my whole being. It's as if I have been released from the burden of carrying something that was never mine to carry. I have my rightful place as second child, first girl in our family, and this knowledge brings with it a lightheaded elation.

The shrink I went to see following the decision to leave my husband and son's father, would understand. Dr Thiolly's "... so she brought you up as a boy" comment in his cabinet in the 16th arrondissement in Paris in 1993 strikes me now as a stunning piece of foresight. I only spent six months visiting his cabinet. I didn't like the fact that my chair was lower than his and told him so. He rectified the "discrepancy." I wasn't willing to feel smaller than I was, nor was I ready to engage in therapy. I went back to see him at the end of 1994 to let him know my brother had "showed up." He was just back from a conference in Canada on family trauma. The focus was the impact that the loss of a child or sibling has on family members, notably mothers. I asked him how he had known. He said he didn't "know" but all the verbal clues had been there. I marvelled at his perspicacity. I didn't know, then, anything about therapeutic techniques that could shine a light on unacknowledged parts of a family system.

I understand, now, why "pink" and "frilly" weren't on offer to me as a little girl; why my hair was cut boyishly short until I was old enough to choose to grow it long. I'm also conscious of the inconsistency in the conclusions I am drawing.

My mother was a skilled dressmaker. She dressed me in beautiful frocks she had made for me. She would dress us both up to go into town on a red bus to Christchurch Central City Square. There was a cathedral in the centre in the square and that's where all the red buses and all the people met. It was a place where you came to shop and smile and wear your best clothes. I have black-and-white photos of my mother and I standing together outside the cathedral, looking very chic in our smart clothes. I remember one dress in particular that I wore to Sunday school. It had puffed sleeves and was gathered at the waist. It was made of a frothy material covered in tiny lemon baubles and tied at the back in a large bow. I wore a stiff petticoat underneath the skirt, which held it out when I walked and crackled when I sat down. The petticoat had a narrow lace hem, which I could run my fingers over when I was sitting down. I loved the dress and the petticoat as much as I loved Sunday school.

To put it simply, I was dressed beautifully as a little girl but raised in the place of a boy.

That was one hell of a fancy act to pull off!

But right now, on a Saturday night in July 1994, the only act to pull off is finding a pub! There are several to choose from, but it's the one with a live band pounding out their '90s version of '80s hits that gets an immediate and unanimous thumbs-up. We push through the swinging doors of the bar and are instantly swallowed up in the thrash and crash; wail and whine of drums and electric guitar backing a sweating vocalist with a voice like Jim Morrison and moves to match. We shake it to the right and we shake to the left. We shake it to the left and we shake it to the right with a vamped-up version of Neal McCoy's "The Shake" country song. We scream "I Love Rock 'n' Roll!" and jump to the band's rendition of the Pointer Sisters' "Jump." Our pelvises gyrate, our fists smash the air, our feet pump out a frenzied rhythm on the wooden floor. We are totally over the top and beyond concern for what "the neighbours" might think. We don't even try to talk. We don't need to talk. Words are superfluous. We are soaked in sweat and hoarse from roaring along with the band. The improbability of our situation lends fire to our thrusting and twirling. We scream with laughter, watching each other dance: brother and sisters, oblivious to the rest of the world, in and outside the pub.

Later, exhausted, after the band has packed up, we cover up and wander down to the beach, reluctant for the night to be over. Now we talk.

We share stories. I tell Ross about the crazy days of Helmore's Lane when I was twenty years old and flatting on the second floor of an old Christchurch house in one of the swankiest neighbourhoods in town; of wild parties and distraught neighbours; of Sunday mornings, crawling out onto the roof through my bedroom window to read the weekend newspaper and eat yoghurt; of my flatmates and their boyfriends; of winter Sunday afternoons watching Monty Python on a small screen; of the utter freedom and insouciance of a time when travel was easy, jobs were a dime a dozen, and careers could be put on hold in order to devote serious time to having fun.

I tell him how I worked in a local dairy every Sunday for two ex-cops who'd decided to go into business together as shop owners and caterers. I make him laugh imagining me in a very short red dress with a white fur bobtail pinned to my bum and long silky-red rabbit ears protruding from the top of my head. He doesn't believe me when I tell him that, dressed as a Bunny Girl, I served the then prime minister of New Zealand, big Norm Kirk, at a workingmen's club celebration in Lyttelton. I make him laugh even more when I describe my boyfriend, dressed up in the same outfit, going into a bar on a Saturday night, on our way to a vice-versa party. He stole the show with his long black fishnet stockings underneath my red silk bunny dress and white floppy ears adorning his shorn head. C sidled up to the bar, batted his false eyelashes, thrust his tennis balls, secured at chest level inside the dress, across the bar top and asked demurely for a beer. Not sure that's what the two ex-cops had in mind as promotional material for their catering business.

I seem to be bent on impressing my brother with

some of my more outrageous exploits as a young woman. I tell him about the time I attended an extra-curricular workshop at the end of my third year at university. There were all kinds of weird and wonderful options available, but I chose to enroll for the half-day cocktail-mixing workshop. It was very much a lips-on affair. We had to taste each concoction to validate the quality of each recipe. You don't need to be a genius to imagine the inebriated scene that emerged from adhering to that sort of scientific approach.

"Thank God it was only a half-day course!" both Maxine and Ross guffaw as one.

"You should have seen the masterful way I manoeuvred my red Honda 50 from the campus back to Helmore's Lane," I boast. Am I competing with him or just showing off? Am I imagining this is how a sister shares "naughty stories" with her brother? He doesn't know what it's like to have a sibling any more than we know what it's like to have a brother. We three are trying on a relationship that we have never worn before.

Ross tells us a bit about his earlier days. There is a chuckle in his voice that makes light of a story that is surely more complex. We can feel his smile warming the night air. His gloveless hands swing easily at his sides as we saunter along the sand.

"I hit the party scene at uni much later than you. I wanted to get out into the world, make some money, do things, you know," he says, looking at us both as if we would understand. Maxine probably does. She had done all sorts of things, including becoming a nurse in Sydney, before she realised art was her life.

"I got married, got a car, got a house, got bored." He bursts out laughing as if recognizing himself too well. We laugh with him. He is infectious. We want to hug him.

"I was no 'office boy'!" It's about the last thing I can imagine him as. I can't see him taking orders from anyone.

"So, I went to night school but that was way too slow for me. Marilyn had a good job, so I went to Otago University full time." I know he must be cutting a few corners here. I know he is no longer married to Marilyn but that she is the mother of his two kids. I don't want to ask him here on the beach, in the light of a clear, king-size moon, after midnight, what happened to his marriage. I don't explain why Christophe's dad is not with me in New Zealand to celebrate my forty-second birthday either.

"Anyway, I got a degree in accounting and became a partner in an accounting firm." He's proud of this achievement. I can hear it in his voice and the way there is a little skip in his step all of a sudden. There is no false modesty about him.

We're entertaining each other, painting our lives in colourful, broad brush strokes. All three of us beam like beacons in the night, reflecting the best of ourselves, as we like to be seen. We are intent on the positive.

JULY 24TH (SUNDAY MORNING)

No one is up very early. We had tiptoed into the house, giggling, in the wee hours of the morning. We had had little to drink but our nocturnal antics had done us in, reminding us that, in fact, we were over forty and not under twenty! Christophe doesn't wake Ross when he slides out of bed and is up early to have breakfast with his grandparents. Ross, Maxine, and I join them at the table when the clatter of plates and the chatter of voices break through our slumber.

Dad teases us about our consumption of alcohol and the racket we made coming in so late. He is really good at creating a relaxed atmosphere with visitors. All three of us have been away for so long that we could all be visitors. He puts on his best bantering self, the way blokes do when they get together. We go along with it, and Ross gives as good as he gets.

As I watch the two of them jockeying for the last word, I wonder how this would have worked had we grown up in the same household. Right now, I'm just enjoying being a spectator, but where would my voice have found its place between the two vying masculine energies? I clashed with my dad whenever I decided to stand up for myself, but looking back, it was a healthy relationship. He dished out old-fashion punishment for serious misbehaviour (like the time I wrecked the neighbours' garden and back porch). I screamed my opposition when I really wanted something he wouldn't grant (like when I needed his permission to go to Australia with an athletics team at age thirteen).

It was a different story with my mother. I sulked silently when I felt she had wronged me, but I wouldn't raise my voice to her. I would have grown into a very different person had I grown up with an older brother. Maybe I wouldn't have been brought into being at all. Maybe I'm only here to cover up a guilty absence. I am free to invent and believe whatever story I wish, but it's not worth the effort, because it didn't happen. I didn't grow up with an elder brother.

Ross, abandoned first and adored second, is insatiably centre stage—larger than life—impossible to ignore. He commands attention and love and receives it in dollops. I, born second and deferred to as first, receive unrequested attention. I do not doubt my importance or my place. That it isn't rightfully mine is a mere quirk of fate right now.

We make plans to meet in Christchurch, where he's currently living with his second wife and her two daughters.

And then it is over. He says goodbye. He takes a taxi back to the airport. And there we all are: mother, father, grandson, sister, and me, just as we were prior to dessert last Thursday evening.

Except that nothing will ever be the same again.

JULY 29TH TO 31ST (THE FOLLOWING WEEKEND)

Ross commutes. He flies to Auckland every Monday morning and returns home to his wife in Christchurch every Friday night.

Christophe and I fly into this household from Napier the week after meeting Ross. We're welcomed with hospitality afforded family members who show up out of the blue needing a bed for the night. We stay several nights and meet the "adopted" whanau—extended family. Is this what Ross does: adopt whanau? It would make sense. How could he not want to make everyone feel welcome into the family? Feeling that your very existence was not welcomed must leave an indelible mark on a psyche. It is not something we can share and I am glad of that. Anyway, my Parisian apartment is too small to squeeze in any extra whanau.

When Ross arrives home on Friday night, he is greeted by soft candlelight and low music that permeate his wife's beautiful old wooden house situated in a discretely luxurious part of the city. He tells me in not so many words that this isn't really his "thing." He says—to me—that he doesn't really feel at home in the atmosphere. I wonder if it's just because it is, literally, not his house but a home he only lives in during the weekends. Or, it could be that the switch from the alpha male world he moves in all week in Auckland to the romance and poetry that greets him at the door on Friday night is just too abrupt? Or, is it that someone else is determining the flow of the evening? I don't know him well enough to pigeonhole him and I just want to go along with the play, whatever it is. I love the atmosphere and I love his wife. She is elegant, sensitive and really intelligent. She has a subtle sense of humour that would be easy to miss in the noise of Kiwi social-ese. I find it easy to talk to her. I discover she is a lawyer. She has fine listening skills that go well with the type of counselling and representation she does. She cares about people. Ross does too, but differently. I can't put my finger on how yet. I wonder how she would feel if Ross told her he would rather arrive home after a harrowing week in Auckland to full lights, feet up, and a beer. From what I have seen of my brother so far, he doesn't appear to be someone who sits down for long. He flits, albeit purposefully, but flits, nevertheless, from one place to another. He doesn't appear to seek stillness and stillness obediently eludes him.

In the weekend that Christophe and I spend at their house in Christchurch, I discover more things about my brother: He can be exhausting! He shows me his car. He shows me his boat. He shows me off to anyone we meet. We meet a lot of people in one weekend. We are always on the go.

And we are laughing most of the time.

For some reason, I never thought to ask my brother what he actually did for a living. I now find out he is a sales manager for Independent Broadcasting. I don't actually know what that means, but if it's sales, he must spend a lot of time "charming" people. I don't really know what he is selling though, and for some reason I don't want to ask—yet. I think I am still starstruck by his presence and in awe of my relationship to him. I notice that he and his wife seem to dance to very different rhythms but assume it's because they live apart all week and it takes time to get in tune again.

During the weekend, I get a call from Mum, whose

voice sounds tight.

"I've got something to tell you."

Her tone suggests regret, but it could also be excitement. I can't decide which it is and am not yet immune to this type of statement. I brace for another curveball. How many siblings can one acquire in the space of a week?

"I was ironing your green silk nightie and I scorched it. Only slightly. I am so sorry."

I am gobsmacked. Thoughts roll out in rapid succession: *How lovely that she is ironing my nightie for me. I can live with a scorched nightie. I can buy another one.*

I was so prepared for another curveball that the adrenaline suddenly dissipates, leaving me feeling weak with relief. *It's only about a nightie!* My head feels light and my throat is dry. I feel rage moving to the surface, like bubbles of a newly opened bottle of champagne. I am metaphorically raising an axe high above my mother's head, ready to execute her for her inability to ascertain the emotional impact on me of telling me she has scorched my nightie and telling me I have had a bona fide brother for the past forty-two years. And for her "confession" of responsibility for both events delivered in the same tone of voice. To my own ears my voice does not betray me. I tell my mother that my nightie will still be wearable, that no one will see the mark in the dark; that it was an accident, that no harm is done.

Despite pretending otherwise, I am blaming her but am not skilled enough or mature enough to read the profuse apology for the scorched nightie as an attempt to say something about the other.

The following questions are invitations to reflect on your own life. They will appear at the end of each of the six parts of this story. My story is not unique. Each one of you has a story to tell. These questions will help you tell that story to someone else. You might like to jot down your responses in the spaces below each question or you may like to engage in a conversation with a friend or family member by asking them the questions. Equally, you may like to skip over them and move on to the next part of the story.

Questions:

What has been THE game changer in your life?

What has this event enabled you to do? Prevented you from doing?

What part of yourself do you really like and want others to like too?

What part of yourself would you rather keep hidden?

Think of a moment of pure joy which held you spellbound in the present moment—what is the abiding memory of that moment?

What kind of relationship do you have with "secrets"?

Can you keep a secret? If you can't, who would you share a secret with?

Are you holding a secret in your heart that burdens you?

Stand next to me when the doorbell rings on July 22nd, 1994. How are you feeling?

> Remember a time when you really wanted to buy a gift for someone you cared about but circumstances made it tricky. How did you get around the problem? How did you feel about the result?

PART TWO

And the Beat Goes On— The Interim Years

A FAMILY WEEKEND IN NAPIER, 1997

I spent time getting to know my brother. I did some crazy things, like organize a business trip to New Zealand on the pretence that I wanted to sell my skills as a trainer to the New Zealand Institute of Management. I set up a series of interviews in Auckland and Wellington and off I flew from Paris, one more time. I met Ross where he was working in Auckland and we wined and dined together in the city, before driving down to Napier for a weekend with the family. My sister joined us, making our family complete for the second time in forty-five years. I don't remember if Dad closed the venetian blinds while we all had breakfast this time, but I do remember we three "kids" giggling and falling onto Mum and Dad's bed together. I don't know what we were playing at, but I do remember feeling deliriously happy.

We dedicated ourselves to putting on an outstanding performance of "Happy Families." We were immaculate in our roles. That Saturday, we drove to Kairakau Beach, eighty kilometres south of the town. No chance of any neighbours spying on us and asking my parents awkward questions. The weather was blue-sky perfect. The beach was golden-sand perfect. The picnic was sausage roll-bacon and egg pie perfect. The sea was dazzle fresh-rolling surf perfect. The only thing that didn't fit the picture-perfect postcard was my chasing my brother down to the water's edge. Neither of us could run the way we would have done—could have done—had we been the kids we were pretending to be. I don't remember what was said during the weekend. I only remember what we did. And then, it was over.

On Monday morning, Ross drove me down to Wellington for another couple of my business meetings. I didn't give a damn about any of these meetings. I had woken up to my subterfuge. I had just wanted to spend time in the exciting company of my brother and this had been the story I had needed to tell myself in order for that to happen.

After the meetings, we met for dinner and subsequently showed up at the hotel I'd booked late in the evening. I invited Ross to share the room with me.

"My brother will be sharing the room with me." I smiled at the receptionist.

"I'll just note his name, Ms Burney." The receptionist returned an immaculate smile while sizing up the situation. He could see a man and a woman of roughly the same age dressed in business attire claiming to be brother and sister. He could see the hour and came to his own conclusions.

"It's Ross McRobie." Ross had a huge grin all over his face. He knew what this looked like. I suddenly saw it too. *Shit!*

"So, it's a Mr McRobie and a Ms Burney for one night in a double room. Is that correct?"

"That's correct. Thank you." I brazened my way through. There was no way I was going to insist that he was my brother. As soon as the elevator doors closed on us, we collapsed into gales of laughter.

"Shit, Bro', you could've been a bit more convincing. You were having a good time down there with the receptionist. Damn you!"

"You weren't exactly convincing, yourself! Anyway, look at the hour. No one's going to buy a story about us being brother and sister. We don't even have the same name."

"I could have given my married name. Who cares, anyway? We have a bed for the night. Well, one of us does!"

We tossed for the bed. Ross slept on the couch and I never did get any business in New Zealand.

And the beat goes on.

THE LETTER, 1998

The phone rings at my home in Paris. It's my mother. She sounds excited.

"You'll never guess what!"

True.

"What?"

"You're not going to believe me."

I probably will.

"There was a letter waiting for us when got back from holiday...."

OMG! I catch my breath and hold it. *It's been four years since we met Ross but surely....?*

No! That's unthinkable. *Don't tell me there's another brother—or—sister who's just shown up.* It has to be another silk nightie story, but why would Mum sound so excited?

"Dad has a brother!"

"What! You have to be kidding me!"

She is not joking—but I feel like roaring with laughter. I can tell she does too. I think she's relieved it's not her on the hook this time. I feel giddy, wondering how many more family members are going to pop up out of the woodwork. I feel unscathed by my discovery of a brother; as if life had rewarded me first prize for second place. I wonder what life has been like in my newfound cousin's family. But I'm not going to find out in the space-time of a long-distance telephone call.

Mum reads me out the contents of the letter, which she tells me has been typewritten on airmail paper and dated March 2nd, her birthday.

Dear Brian,

To say that life is full of surprises is, to my way of thinking, a gross understatement when, thanks to my daughter Adrienne and her genealogy exercise, I find that I have another family I knew nothing about. It is a sad fact of life that when we were born the word 'adoption' had a certain stigma about it, was always used in hushed tones and whispers, and there was the expression 'He mustn't be told.' My stepbrothers and stepsister[1] were sworn to secrecy, but I feel I should have been told everything when my adoptive mother died in 1941; however, that didn't happen. I must state, however, that I was brought up in a loving/caring environment in Christchurch, given a good education, and really lacked for nothing.

I recall that during the '30s, while learning the piano, I was taken many times to Lyttelton to visit the Bradley family and acquired some sheet music showing the name Melva Bradley I suspected nothing. Further, it

---

[1] Theo had been adopted by a recently married couple in their forties. The wife had been a widow with three teenage children. Her children were Theo's adopted brothers and sister as well as being his stepsiblings.

really saddens me to realise that during service in the RNZAF, I was stationed at Woodbourne, mid-1964 to mid-1967, and was unaware that my birth mother and some of her family lived nearby. Now, I am truly amazed and 'chuffed' to find I have a half brother and two half-sisters.

A lot of time has been wasted, but I would like to think we could correspond from time to time, and eventually meet up.

Finally, I hope you will accept this typewritten letter, as my handwriting leaves a lot to be desired. Also, I have 'xeroxed' this letter so that you all are told the same things at the same time.

Sincerely, in anticipation,

Theo Moreton

PS: Brian,
I was Nav. on a Catalina, Jan to Aug 1946, which was captained by a Dave Regan, I believe. Was a grocer in Levin. Know him?

When Mum finishes reading out my uncle Theo's letter to his brother, my dad, I am stunned by its pathos, by the terribly ordinary tragedy of our lives. I've lost my initial desire to laugh at the irony of my father discovering that he too has acquired a secret sibling. My grandmother achieved what Mum could not, a generation later, which was to go to her grave without revealing her secret. I suspect Mum feels the ground has been levelled between her and her mother-in-law. I'm blown away by the power of shame to wreak havoc on a family system by silencing voices and provoking pain that cannot find its right name. And, I have to remember that the first birth control clinic only opened in Auckland in 1953. That the pill only became available in 1961 and then, only for married women. That abortion was an act of criminality in 1961. By the time I was eighteen and had decided to divest of my virginity, I knew about the pill and what happened if you didn't have safe sex. I went to see our family doctor. In secret. I wanted to be very adult but felt so embarrassed and ashamed of my request that I went mute once I got into his surgery.[2] He looked at me. I blushed furiously. He scribbled a couple of words on a slip of paper and slid it across his desk. It read, "The pill?" I lowered my eyes and smiled sheepishly. "Yes," I whispered. I never looked back! Unlike the women of my grandmother's and mother's generation, who were condemned socially while being deprived of any acceptable options. It's so easy to take freedom for granted when you don't know what came before your time.

---

[2] In New Zealand a doctor's office or consulting room is called a surgery.

I don't remember how the conversation with my mother ended, but I do know she did not read me out Dad's reply to his newfound brother's letter. I can't recall us ever really discussing the topic. I never asked my dad about his brother or how he felt when he opened Theo's letter in 1998. I don't know why. Even though the two cats were out of their respective bags, I still sensed Ross and Theo remained taboo conversation items in my parents' presence; apart or together.

THE REPLY, 2022

It was Boxing Day 2022. Dad had been dead for twelve years already when I finally got to read my father's reply to his brother. I was back in New Zealand one more time, getting closure on family affairs. My sister and I were visiting our cousin, Adrienne, and her mother, Chris, at their place in Aidanfield, Christchurch. It was after the tea had been poured that Adrienne pulled out her treasure trove of amassed family history, including correspondence between Dad and his brother. I read the initial letter from Theo again, before reading Dad's reply. His letter was handwritten in blue biro, the words sprawled across two pages of lined paper. It was dated March 8th, 1998. The date told me Dad responded immediately to Theo's first letter.

Dear Theo,

> It was good to get your letter and hear a bit about another side of the family. It is also a big surprise to find out you are not the eldest; our mother was a surprise also....

Well, Dad, no shit! I thought back to that birthday dinner in July 1994, when Dad gave us the news about Ross.

I pore over Dad's handwriting, trying to decipher some of the words. I handle the letter as a precious document—as though I am a privileged eavesdropper on their conversation. I feel it is Dad's authentic self that is moving his hand. Like his brother, he gives information and I, the reader, am left to sense what the two men must have felt meeting each other on the page after *seventy years* of absence.

Both are New Zealand men of colonial descent who came of age during wartime: one an airman, the other a seaman. Both are circumspect in the expression of their feelings, sticking to simple facts:

> Interesting to hear you were stationed in Woodbourne [Airbase] with Mum and the girls living so handy but that's life. I never lived in Blenheim, the family shifted there when I was in the Navy and the only time spent there was on leave.

Working my way through Dad's words, I sense an undercurrent of apology for being the one who was kept; of a younger brother scrambling to catch up with his older sibling by putting distance between himself and the mother who gave birth to them both. But he also writes, in the next paragraph,

> It sounds as though you follow Mum's line with the piano. She was always good, but I do not think I appreciated it.

Is he telling his older brother, "You got something from her I never got?" Is my dad trying to rebalance the scales?

Dad tells his brother, "My service was as a seaman from August 1945 to January 1952." He writes Theo that he trained as seaman in Taranaki and then "joined the *Achilles* and went back to the UK on her, then we brought the *Bellona* out. Our path could have crossed with you in the sky." Dad could be saying that the two of them are worlds apart, but I feel that it is more his way of intimating relationship. In his next sentence, he observes that Theo's career in the Airforce "sounds interesting" and acknowledges that he "obviously did well."

What can you get onto two pages on a Sunday morning in March 1998, one week after you've discovered you have an older brother? Mine, at least, came for the weekend.

He then switches the topic by asking, "Are you tall? Mum's brothers all were, but I seem to have been left behind at 5 [foot] 11 [inches]." I am reminded of the first conversation with Ross, my own brother, and the slightly delirious sensation I had of jumping from pillar to post in an attempt to get to know him and not really knowing where to start.

Dad responds to Theo's query about Dave Regan, the former naval captain and now grocer in Levin.

> Although we live in Levin, it is new country to us, so your pal Captain Dave Regan's name does not mean anything to me.

Dad then jumps to his own working life in the administration of public hospitals in three different parts of the country. He concludes, "When I retired, it was a great service with great people, but it has now all gone." It's true. Since deregulation in New Zealand in the 1980s, public services and notably the hospital system has radically changed—but is Dad also sharing a sense of time lost with his brother?

He tells Theo he only has vague memories of Lyttelton, where Theo was taken as a child to visit the Bradley family—to the house on the hill where his grandparents lived—where he was given his mother's sheet music with the name, her name, Melva, written on it. Dad writes that his father was a blacksmith and "I vaguely remember old granddad with his big moustache." He says that their common maternal grandmother, Gran, was "a little person."

What did the grandparents say to one another after the child Theo had taken leave of the house and the piano lesson? Did they say, "Melva's boy is growing into a fine young lad?" Or, "He's just like his mother—good at the piano?"

Was Melva present for these visits?

How did she feel looking at her son?

Was she ever tempted to confess, or was the power of the family taboo too strong?

Where was the father?

Did Theo ever meet Lil, the baby girl the Bradleys adopted into the family six months after Theo was adopted out of it?

What on earth was going on in my great grandparents' household? There is so much left unsaid in these two letters. And so much no one will ever know now.

I go back to Theo's initial "letter of introduction" and read the postscripts to his two sisters that he has scribbled over on the copy to my dad. To his sister Dawn, he remarks, "Raylene left for the USA last Friday, soon to become Mrs Hansen. COINCIDENCE."

"Hansen" is Dad's sister's married name.

In his second postscript to his other sister, Jan, he writes, "Another coincidence—Adrienne's middle name is Jan, while Chris's middle name is Lorraine!"

Adrienne is Theo's eldest daughter, my cousin. Chris is the name of Theo's wife. Lorraine is the name given to my aunt's daughter.

Like Theo, I am struck by these strange "coincidences." These names are like silk threads weaving Theo loosely into the fabric of his family of origin. Theo claims he was brought up in a loving household, while Dad is dismissive of his own.

Who loses or gains the most: the kept ones or the abandoned ones? Joining the world has all the attributes of a wretchedly marvellous sweepstake. Looking at this from the outside whilst remaining firmly on the inside leaves me with a feeling of helplessness but not hopelessness. I am just another microscopic creature taking part in a gigantic drama that didn't start with me and won't stop with me.

Dad concludes his letter to Theo by saying he's not too keen on crossing Cook Strait to visit his brother in Nelson but writes, "If you wish, we have room here and you would be most welcome." He signs it, "Sincerely, Brian."

Whatever slant I give to Dad's words, it is clear by

the overall tone of the letter that he is happy to have a brother, just as I was. I never met my Uncle Theo and don't recall my dad ever mentioning his brother to me. But then, he did maintain his lifelong habit of repeating the old English proverb: "Children should be seen and not heard." Maybe he learnt it from his mother. It was and is a very effective means of quelling a child's curiosity, and once the child has acquired the habit of not speaking to her parents, she simply then never thinks to ask even the most obvious questions like, "How was it for you when you met your brother?" and "What did you talk about?"

We both had brothers we didn't grow up with. He met his when he was seventy and was too old to enjoy much of his company, given they lived on different islands. I met mine, his son, when I was forty-two and had twenty-seven years to enjoy his company even though we lived in different hemispheres. Both my grandmother and my mother suffered from the times they made love in. Both their families supported the secrets their daughters kept from the children who followed. The secrets were a source of pain to one family and a source of joy to another.

And the beat goes on.

CHRISTMAS IN LEVIN, 1999

I introduced my partner, Richard, (the one I had left my husband for) to New Zealand and my family in December 1999. "Family," by this time, was an expansive term. When I'd first met Richard, I had a sister and nine cousins on both sides of the family. By the time he set foot on my home soil at the end of the twentieth century, the family had grown to include a brother, a sister-in-law, a niece and a nephew, an uncle, and several cousins I had yet to meet.

It was an auspicious moment to introduce Richard to New Zealand. The sun was going to rise over the twenty-first century there, twelve hours ahead of Europe and we wanted to be amongst the lucky few. If the world was going to shut down at the stroke of midnight, as speculated upon in the media, then we would be amongst the first to know what that would look like. The millenium bug was predicted to be to the computer what COVID would later be to the human race: an unmitigated disaster. Ross had invited us to share the end of the world, at the bottom of the world, with him and his wife.

We flew into Auckland a few days before Christmas and travelled south to Levin. Maxine joined us on Christmas Eve. Richard had no difficulty adapting to the novelty of a Christmas season in shorts and T-shirt but was unprepared for the culture shock of his first Christmas lunch Down Under. My mother had booked us into a restaurant by the beach. It had a reputation of serving fresh crayfish straight from the sea-pot to the table. She wanted it to be a taste of the "real" New Zealand—something special for Richard's first visit to the country.

The treat didn't start well when the day dawned cold and windy. Determined to be true to the myth of the intrepid Kiwi, unfazed by a bit of weather, we donned summer clothes, brave smiles, and headed off for lunch, Richard in tow.

After checking the address several times, we were forced to conclude that the slightly upmarket-of-a-shack before us was indeed, the restaurant. It was a red-painted wooden take-away with a corrugated iron roof and was plonked on the side of the road with a couple of matching wooden picnic tables and benches nearby. Mum looked taken back. Maxine didn't bat an eye and Dad looked unfazed. I tittered. No one looked at Richard. In we went.

The walls were covered in painted murals depicting sailing boats bobbing on white-capped, deep azure seas. They sailed beneath dazzling blue skies dotted with white candy-floss clouds. The Christmas tree draped in red tinsel and dripping baubles in the corner of the room declared the season and the reason for our visit. There were already people seated at the trestle tables that ran in rows across the restaurant.

Absolutely my mother's sense of aesthetics. I looked at Mum without needing to say anything. We both raised an eyebrow and I wondered how we would play this: "This is how we do Christmas in NZ" or "We thought you might like to experience something different for your first Christmas in NZ" or "OMG, this isn't happening!"

Richard whispered in my ear, "Seriously?" with a quizzical look on his face.

I couldn't resist the opportunity for a bit of a tease.

"It's my mother's favourite restaurant. She comes here all the time," I said, ostentatiously, with a huge grin. The tension broke and Mum burst out laughing. Dad wondered what the joke was and Maxine just giggled, embarrassed, unsure if I was joking or being sarcastic. Richard picked up the flavour of my humour and relaxed into the low-key, friendly atmosphere inside the takeaway.

Most of the men were in my dad's age bracket and wore traditional Kiwi summer attire of Bermuda shorts and long socks to just below the knee. The ladies wore summer dresses and cardigans. My mother stood out from the other women of her age in her elegant grey slacks and silky, long-sleeved white blouse. I noticed there were no young families or children here and understood that this place, on this particular day, wasn't just about the fresh cray. Once I stopped looking down my nose at the décor, I could see its true value. People had gathered here to be together and the fresh cray was a bonus. Christmas could be a devastatingly lonely time of the year for some people.

I remembered the first Christmas after I had left my husband. It was disastrous. I had locked myself out of my apartment in Paris and left the car keys inside. I had no way of getting hold of a spare set on Christmas Day so had walked the five kilometres back to the flat I'd left the previous summer. It was freezing and no one had mobile phones back then, so I couldn't call my ex to ask for help. I cried all the way but smiled bravely when my ex gave me a photo of the PC that hadn't arrived on time for it to be my Christmas present. Our son didn't understand anything but felt everything. We made the best of a bad job by pretending to be joyful. It was a horrendous experience for all three of us. We never repeated the "exercise;" Christmas was left to die an unnatural death on the altar of a broken family.

At a beach ten kilometres east of Levin, on a cold summer's day in 1999, I didn't know who any of the people were, or what their stories were. Maybe they had indeed chosen to be there just for the fresh cray but, looking at the age bracket, I thought it more likely that it was for the undemanding company of strangers.

We took our places at one of the trestle tables at the back of the room and introduced ourselves to the other "strangers" already sitting there. I was curious to know why they were there but chose to respect the bonhomie the season demanded, so left my questions under the table.

The tables were covered in dark red crepe paper and decorated with small sprigs of gold-painted pine. I caught Richard's eye and winked at him. "Not quite what you're used to, eh?" I whispered, thinking back to my own first Christmas Eve in France in 1978. I had packed bags and left London to join my girlfriend Lynn in Paris. She'd asked me to look after her cat while she went back to New Zealand to marry the Frenchman she'd met in Tehran. The man in question just happened to be the son of the curator of Le Louvre at the time. I'd arrived in Paris by bus with all my worldly possessions in tow, including a teddy bear and a giant rubber plant. I was taken to a grand old apartment in the 16th arrondissement to share their Christmas Eve meal with Madame and her grown children.

I had entered into battle with a raw oyster which,

despite all the attacks I made on it with my fork, had stubbornly refused to budge from its shell. "Lack of practice," I had muttered between clenched teeth. My hosts had looked on, discreetly, with an air of quiet dismay. I compounded my "gaucheness" by slicing the camembert instead of cutting it in a wedge. The oyster debacle should have been warning enough for my hosts but no, they insisted on serving the cheese to me first out of sheer politeness. They proffered the crusty wheel with no operating guidelines. I sliced! I felt a long way, then, from home. A long way from the roast lamb, green peas and roast potatoes served on Christmas Day at lunchtime during my childhood in New Zealand.

Meanwhile, back at the shack, Bing Crosby's "I'm Dreaming of a White Christmas" was adding a festive air to the occasion as we made our way up to the serving table and took our place in the queue. Bing and Frank Sinatra and their "snow" songs were dopamine triggers for me and judging by the hums and smiles around me, I wasn't the only one cruising in the feel-good zone.

As a child, it had never struck me as odd that we would eat a winter roast in the middle of summer, or decorate the shop windows with cottonwool balls in imitation of snow, or sing Christmas carols about decking the halls with holly, or never wonder why Father Christmas sweated inside his big red suit and long white beard. It wasn't until I went to Munich for Christmas in 1980 that I saw huge fir trees dripping snow in the streets. I saw children being pulled over snow-covered ground in real sleighs. My breath made white puffs in the night air. Santa Claus kept himself warm in his big woolly red suit. The Christmas tree in my in-laws' lounge was alight with tiny, but real, candles. The glittery cards my mother had written inside and sent diligently to family and friends every Christmas had come true. It was like discovering the world of Disney was full of real people and not just the cartoons of talking ducks and mice.

We were a long way in time and space from Munich 1980 and even further from a German or French way of "doing" Christmas dinner. This was lunch for one thing and for another, it was a self-service, come-as-you-are, eat-as-much-as-you-want affair. There were plates piled high with cooked vegetables and potatoes; salads and desserts. There was a large, ruddy-faced man, wearing a bloodstained butcher's apron, wielding a large carving knife, standing behind the serving table. He would have been terrifying had he not been beaming and "Ho Ho Ho-ing" at everyone who tendered their plate. The red woolly suit would have looked good on him. He sliced roasted lamb off the bone and loaded it onto our plates, wished us a Merry Christmas, and indicated fresh cray on the large serving platters next to the lamb, just begging to be eaten.

Richard was looking flummoxed. "When in Rome," I said out of the corner of my mouth. OK, so it didn't fit with his idea of French culinary etiquette but then, I would never have thought to serve roast lamb with crayfish either. *What the hell*, I thought, *tell me the last time you could afford to eat crayfish to your heart's content? Certainly not in France—and certainly not in 1999.*

To this day, my sister insists that I, alone, ate three whole crayfish. She's lying, of course. I don't remember who ate what, how much, or in what order, but I do remember that it was superb, plentiful, unpretentious, and inexpensive.

And the beat goes on.

Y2K IN WANAKA

Richard had just about come to terms with life Down Under by the time we reached Lake Wanaka in the far south of New Zealand on the last day of the century. He had managed to get a jar of fine-quality goose-liver pate from France into the country without losing it at the border to a zealous customs officer. On arrival in Wanaka, he proudly gifted it to Ross, who beamed his pleasure and offered to serve it with coffee for breakfast—the equivalent of my slicing the side off the camembert! Richard just looked at him, wondering what to make of this famous brother of mine whom he was meeting for the first time.

"Il plaisante?" Richard whispered, eyebrows raised in my direction.

"Non," I whispered back. "He can't read the label. It's in French!" Thinking how well I had just handled my first diplomatic mission between the two men, I remembered the camembert incident. "Wedged or sliced, it's all bloody cheese," I had wanted to grumble at the time. I could hear Ross taking a dig at Richard's "Frenchiness": "Bit touchy about liver pate, are we, Richard?" I could see Richard rolling his eyes like his fellow countrymen and thinking there was no hope for "les sauvages." The French tended to be "sensitive" if not downright arrogant when it came to the how and when and what of eating. Not wise to mess with a Frenchman and his foie gras! Not good to serve it with coffee for breakfast either. Well, not in the France as it was at the turn of the century.

I smiled brightly at Ross and said, "We're both tea drinkers, but you go ahead and have some with your coffee. We'd be happy to share some with you on a bit of toast, before dinner on New Year's Day with a glass of wine."

I sent a wink Richard's way and thought I should

put in an application for a position in an international diplomacy department.

We got on to more familiar territory, at least for Ross, when we started packing up his motorboat for our New Year celebration up the lake. I was quite excited anticipating a very different New Year from all our friends back in France. I noticed, though, that Ross and A, his wife, were not saying much to each other and when either of them did speak, it was in clipped terms. There was a lot to do, so I assumed the brevity of their exchanges was due to the stress of the moment. The last day of the year was overcast and it didn't seem like we'd be amongst the lucky few to actually see the sun rise over a new century. By four o'clock the boat was packed and attached to the SUV. We shared the back seat of the car with the Chow. I wasn't fond of dogs at the best times. My experience led me to judge them all as drooling, barking, erratic, smelly creatures. Ross's Chow, however, sat quietly aloof in a corner, minding his own business.

He's a giant cat, I thought. *If only dogs were more like cats.* I sighed, settling into the opposite corner of the car.

I don't remember the name of the island we anchored at, nor exactly when it started to drizzle, but I do remember a dismal feeling of being marooned in the middle of nowhere at the end of the century. If the world was going to grind to a halt at midnight, I didn't want to be in a tent, up a lake, at the bottom of the world.

Although, thinking about it, that could have its advantages.

Ross and A did most of the work while Richard and I lamely handed over tent pegs and the odd barbecue utensil. Despite my origins, I'd had very little experience camping. The makeshift nature of camp life wouldn't have appealed to my mother and, possibly, the initial outlay for all the equipment would have been prohibitive. I was city (albeit small city) born and bred so felt more than useless as my brother and his wife went about setting up camp for the big night.

I remained cheerfully determined to celebrate the end of the century or the world or both, come what may. Standing on that quiet patch of rock lulled by the gentle sound of water lapping the shore, the threatened apocalypse felt like centuries rather than just hours away.

The tension between our camp "Mum 'n' Dad" did not ease. It felt familiar; you could have sliced the silence with a meat knife during dinnertimes when I was growing up. I didn't know what was going on between Ross and A but it was obvious they were not happy. Maybe A didn't like camping and was missing her beautiful old house and candlelit evenings in Christchurch. I felt I owed my loyalty to Ross so didn't make any enquiries into A's well-being.

"Did you pack the blow-up mattresses?" A asked Ross out of the blue.

"No, I thought you did!" he snapped back.

"I thought you were doing it." His wife gave a limp smile and shrugged.

"No, dear, that was your job. I have thought of everything else." Ross's jaw stiffened.

I wasn't about to risk a drama triangle scenario by stepping in with any soothing comments. Not only was this patch of beach stony under foot, it was now going to be stony under back. I tried to remember why Richard and I had been so seduced by the romance of seeing in the century turn in this part of the world. It hadn't ticked any of the boxes so far.

I don't remember what we ate around the campfire, which had a hard time staying alight, but I do know I was wearing waterproof gear over shorts and T-shirt. Caught between a rock and a hard place, I easily stayed awake until the countdown to midnight. The anticipated firework display of mega proportions was nothing more than a lame fizzle of light shooting into a moonless sky on the stroke of midnight.

Having done our duty of seeing in the New Year, we crawled into the tent and lay down on the hard ground to fiddle with sleep. The Chow settled between A and Ross on one side and Richard and I on the other. His fur was damp and he was large. He snuffled and snorted, disgruntled, I supposed, with the sleeping arrangements. Ross barked a couple of master-to-dog commands and the dog dropped his head onto his front paws.

"I'll let you know when we're having a good time," I whispered, in French, to Richard.

And so began the new millennium: flat on my back on stony ground, next to a soggy dog, in a tent, up a lake, at the bottom of the world, under a sodden sky. The sun was still sulking when daylight broke a few hours later. I took a picture of Richard coming out of the tent, still in his wet-weather gear but wearing a valiant smile that belied the desperate look in his eye. The caption beneath the photo would read: "How I survived my first trip to New Zealand."

At least the drizzle had let up, so I helped the Bro' barbecue up a breakfast of sausages, eggs, and bacon for us all. Life was good. I was upright. I was dry. I had food on my plate. AND best of all, I no longer had to pretend to be having a good time. The famous damn end-of-century celebration was over. Nothing untoward had happened to the world, as far as I could tell. I regretted that there was no opportunity to speak to

Ross on his own. I wanted to find out what was going on between him and A. Together, as a foursome, there was little to say. Talking was confined to what had to be done next. Once breakfast was over, the whole process started in the reverse. We took down the tent, packed up the boat and, Ross at the helm, sped back to the township of Wanaka. I sat at the back of the boat, thrilling to the roar and froth of cutting through water at speed. I felt complicit in the pleasure I sensed my brother was getting out of holding the fast wide curves under control. While we were engaged in motion, talking was superfluous. It crossed my mind that he was probably someone who never got caught with himself alone. In a group, we were all part of an endless show.

Unpacked—one more time—back at the Warren Street bach,[3] we turned on the TV, took out the foie gras, poured some wine, and watched the extraordinary fire-work displays in the world's major cities. In the comfort and dry of the lounge, we chuckled at our futile attempt to celebrate this momentous event and noted ironically, "Well, the TV is working—it can't all be bad news!"

The world went on and our computers didn't let us down. Ross's relationship with A went on for another

---

[3] A bach is a second house usually in a beach or lake area. It is usually rough and ready.

four months. He and A did indeed dance to a different tune. He wanted to feel he had a woman behind everything he did, and she needed emotional security. I didn't need a diploma in therapy to figure out which woman he wanted to feel behind him. It was no surprise to learn that he had met someone else shortly after everyone returned to work in January. True to form, Ross didn't muck around when he wanted something—or someone. He set the goal and got the goal. He didn't let anything stand in his way. The woman he wanted was also in an unhappy marriage. It was none of my business. I was certainly not in a position to judge, given that I too had left a husband, wanting to be true to myself regardless of the fallout to my son and husband. I understood the existential necessity to quest happiness—or at least, honesty in a relationship.

Ross left A, and I lost a kindred spirit. I went to see her in her office a few years later when all the messy bits of the divorce were over and done with. It was all polite smiles and awkward conversation. I made no further attempt to bridge the abyss, but Ross never gave up trying to re-include A in his life. Excluding anyone from his orbit was not part of his DNA. He made several attempts over time to patch his former marriage into a friendship. He had managed the feat with his first wife and mother of his children. But A steadfastly wanted nothing more to do with him. No amount of charm or goodwill could repair the damage his infidelity had inflicted on her. She had already been an emotionally injured woman when he married her, so his leaving her had gouged a wound that could bear no further touching.

Ross bore her no ill will, just as I bore my first husband no ill will, but both Ross and I were in the privileged position of going towards love while leaving a former loved one like a dirty sock dropped beside the laundry basket.

And the beat goes on.

ANOTHER ONE OF THOSE PHONE CALLS

When my son called in late 2010 to announce he was getting married, I gasped. When he announced in his second sentence that he was converting to Judaism, I gulped.

"So, you've found your spiritual path." It was a lame attempt to disguise my shock.

I hadn't seen that one coming. I remember when he was at the end of his schooling and we were walking along the street together, discussing future options. He turned to me and said he was thinking about joining an elite combat force. I did not scream, "Are you off your rocker?" I calmly took a slow, deep breath and said with as much enthusiasm as I could fake, "That's an interesting idea. Where could you get more information on what the requirements are for joining?" Maybe the kid that he was inside wanted to shock his mother into some kind of radical refusal of his idea that he could fight against. I had always held the belief that it was better to discuss and explore rather than oppose and reject my son's ideas outright. When he announced that he was converting to Judaism, I maintained the same policy.

"I'm joining a community with a history." *He sounds clear and determined. It's not about religion.*

'A community with a history'—that's an understatement! And your name is Christophe. That should go down well with a Jewish community. An assortment of judgmental thoughts avoided expression as I scrambled for my next "Modern Mum" phrase. When the emotional stakes are high, my fallback position is to get the facts. Just as I had on the evening of July 21st, 1994, when I asked a "when" question. Back in 1994, the question had given me recovery-from-shock time. Faced with my son's decision to marry and convert, I asked "when" to keep me safe from letting my disappointment show up as itself or, worse, as criticism. He was marrying his high school sweetheart—but she was not my choice. He was

joining her religious tradition. It was not mine.

His father and I had given him no religious education. His father, born into the Catholic faith, was violently opposed to any "indoctrination" from the church. I had been brought up in a Protestant tradition and couldn't think of any reason to object. I remembered my own father's first reaction to my telling him I was going to marry a Frenchman. "So, you're marrying a Mick." The thought that religion had any bearing on getting married, or that there was an automatic association between a Frenchman and Catholicism, had astonished me. Two generations on and my son was astonishing me with a confirmation that, yes, religion did have something to do with getting married. Much later, I would understand that our son reproached us for not providing the structural guidelines that a religious practice would have given him. We had always told ourselves we were keeping his mind free of prejudice, so he could make an informed choice later. We should not have been surprised when he did exactly that: make an informed, conscious choice. It just wasn't our choice.

It is hard to get child-rearing right. The choices are not obvious. Follow loyally in your parents' footsteps and do as you were done to? Make a stab at rebellion and swear never to repeat the mistakes they made with you? Wobble valiantly between a desire to honour both your spouse's family lore and your own? Ignore your family of origin and embrace your spouse's wholeheartedly? Give up on both sides and claim originality? Whatever it is you think you are doing as a parent, somehow your child has to break loose his bond to you and become his own person. Then he is free to make his own mistakes and you can wring your hands, wondering where you went wrong!

Wrong or right, our son did the training, got circumcised, and was ready to get married in July 2012. I met the rabbi. He was a little guy with a heart that oozed love and a sharp, merry intelligence. He cruised easily between the English, French, and Hebrew languages, couching the great teachings of the Torah in accessible terms for the layperson. I could understand what had attracted my son to him—why he had said "yes" to conversion which, in turn, had facilitated the "yes" to his choice of partner.

During my son's training-to-become-Jewish period, I did my own "training." I remember very clearly a phrase that came to me during a silent meditation early one morning during that time: "You can choose to love her." From that moment onwards, I heeded that inner voice. I did indeed vow to love my future daughter-in-law, come what may. That decision stood me in good stead for the many, as yet unknown, challenges.

To my amazement, I discovered that my son and future daughter-in-law wanted a wedding with over a hundred and fifty people attending. They wanted it white and they wanted it Jewish. They wanted a chocolate fountain and they wanted a champagne tower. They wanted a macaroon mountain and they wanted a chuppah. I didn't have a clue what they were talking about, although the idea of a champagne tower did appeal.

What's a chocolate fountain when it's at home? I conjured up pictures of towers and mountains and fountains and realised there were huge gaps in my education. I should have studied architecture rather than literature.

I began to understand what all the "landscaping" meant when they showed me the figures. A less-hardy person would have gone into immediate cardiac arrest on being informed of what her financial contribution to the "architecture" was to be.

Big white weddings were a new phenomenon for me. The late hippie generation, which I was part of, eschewed them as something that demeaned women. The handing over of the "meringue" from father to husband had been replaced by creative events that took place on beaches, in gardens, up trees—anywhere but a church. The scripts were mutually written by bride and groom requiring only the presence of a justice of the peace to pronounce a couple of legal phrases that sealed the deal. I didn't know what had provoked the swing back to traditional weddings. Women were emancipated, so the choice was all theirs. Men had nothing to fight for—or against—on the matter of marriage, so their role in the planning of a wedding remained perfunctory. According to me. My thoughts may have been influenced by a state of post-traumatic shock brought on by the exorbitant cost of the event my son and his wife-to-be were planning. But the bottom line was, if I wanted the role of mother-of-the-groom, there was a price to pay. I only had one child and definitely wanted "in" so I broke open the piggy bank and went the whole hog.

I would celebrate both my sixtieth birthday and my twenty-nine-year-old son's wedding in one big extravaganza. I invited my New Zealand family to France to share in the party. We would go down to a villa in the south of France at the end of June and come back up to Paris for the wedding in a posh farmhouse in Normandy at the beginning of July. In for a penny, in for a pound!

And the beat goes on.

A BIRTHDAY PARTY, JUNE 2012

It was the first time both my brother and sister would be with me, in person, to celebrate a birthday. We three travelled with our partners in a first-class carriage on a high-speed train down to Avignon on Friday morning, June 22nd. We picked up rental cars and drove to a small hamlet on the outskirts of Uzes. I don't remember much about getting there but do remember that the weather behaved impeccably with no hint of anything but luminous blue and whispering breezes the entire weekend. And I can still recall the delighted squeals when, one by one, my family members pushed past a heavy wooden door in an old stone wall and stepped into a garden of olive trees and flowering lavender bushes. It was like entering a parallel universe. On one side of the hole in the wall was an unassuming sleepy little hamlet and on the other, luxuriant plant life and stone stairways, leading to boutique bedrooms with ensuites that held giant granite bathtubs and step-in showers that were half the size of Richard's and my apartment in Paris. A generous swimming pool sat at the edge of a panoramic view of vineyards and distant hills. Water, space, stone, cicadas, and the fragrance of lavender cast their gentle spell of enchantment over the three-day party. I was in the driver's seat all weekend as Birthday Girl. That was something new for Ross. He wasn't used to being a passenger. We played our inversed roles well.

We took breakfast on a terrace, which was an extension of a huge, open-plan kitchen. We sat under a shade sail made of natural fibre. While I don't recall exactly what we ate, words like "exotic" and "copious" pop up easily. On Saturday morning, we drove into the old town of Uzes. It was market day. The narrow streets and central square were crowded with stalls and people. We tried on hats and lingered to listen to street bands. We snacked on the hoof and came away wearing Panama hats and carrying CDs. We loafed beside the pool in the afternoon and got spruced and coiffed to greet the rest of my birthday guests for champagne at six.

Ross and I were dressed alike, all in black. He looked racy in his plain black T-shirt and trousers. I felt very spiffy in a calf-length fitted crepe skirt with flared edge and matching black top that zipped at the side and laced at the back. Everyone else looked poolside chic in casually elegant clothes and summer footwear. Richard wore his new Panama hat. I basked in the warmth of a birthday ritual of toasts and speeches proclaiming how wonderful I was, how great I looked, and how pleased everyone was to be there.

This beats therapy, I thought, abandoning myself

entirely to the pleasure of the moment. *Not great for the bank balance but right now, who cares?*

Like Ross, I was a planner, not a worrier. I had put a lot of thought into the weekend before it happened so felt free to revel in the fizzing of champagne and the brush of a breeze in my hair. It was my birthday, albeit an early one, and my only child was getting married in a week's time. My friends and family had all said "yes!" My joy in the moment was untainted despite the fact that I knew Henri, husband of Beatrice and both very dear friends from Marseille, was dying of cancer and had very little time left. I recognised what a mega physical effort it was costing him to be there, even with the support of his wife. But sadness could wait in the wings. Its turn for centre stage would come soon enough. I wasn't a Pollyanna. I had sometimes thought my mother was one, given her determination to live according to her mantra, "It won't rain," when every weather forecast said the opposite. I wondered if Ross was a bit of a Pollyanna or if problems were simply marvellous opportunities to find solutions. Personally, I didn't like problems, hence the importance of planning.

I had spent a lot of time doing just that when it came to deciding on the seating arrangements for the Saturday evening dinner. The restaurant owner had responded to my request to have everyone around the same table by creating a huge square that enabled us to sit three guests on each side of the table. It was a perfect number for a perfect structure. I loved a square more than a circle. There was something very pleasing about a straight line. I remember a very old friend of mine teasing me once about my predilection for "straightness." We were co-facilitating a corporate team building event in a fancy hotel in the south of France and preparing for the day by taking an early-morning swim in the hotel pool. She zigzagged slowly around the pool, enjoying the creative possibilities its shape offered. I found the longest stretch of "straight" water and determinedly made my way up and down, clearly signalling I was not to be interrupted. She voiced her stupefaction afterward, telling me, "You are the only person I know who can manage to swim in a straight line in a kidney-shaped pool!"

We still chuckle about that personality trait that contrasts, on the surface, with her own. It's not the whole story but I can't deny my love of straight lines.

So, I was delighted with the square table and my seating arrangements. The party would go swimmingly.

She's English and he dotes on his English heritage.

Both he and she share a trade union background and both are feisty left-wingers. They've both held positions of power in large organizations. They are both native French speakers.

She has a sharp wit and he is a wild extravert. They will support the valiant Henri.

He has the same form of intelligence and sensitivity as her. They will listen to each other's silence as much as their words.

I will sit between my brother and sister, delightfully and, rightfully at the head of the table.

My thinking proved to be correct as I watched people engaging easily in tête-à-tête conversations. I congratulated myself on my cocktail of introverts and extraverts. The extraverts competed with each other for centre stage and kept the party alive late into the night. The introverts dropped the odd sly comment into the mix that got everyone's attention but, in general, they were happy to follow rather than lead. I don't remember exactly what we ate, but we were served lots of small gourmet culinary creations with wild names. Each dish came with a different wine. It was all exquisite. I don't remember what we talked about but there was lots of laughter and banter, a peacock crying, a shoe masquerading as a mobile telephone, a lot of teasing around the number six, more toasts and more speeches. I do remember insisting that we all sing along to the Byrds' version of "Turn, Turn, Turn." Only a true friend would agree to warble through the biblical lyrics: "For everything there is a season" accompanied by static music coming from an underpowered mobile phone, and in a foreign language for half the party. Only good friends could present me with a lemon tree in a pot and trust me to see the funny side of taking it back to Paris. What else would you give a Parisian New Zealander when in the south of France? Of course I would find a way to take it home on the train with me. One does.

And the beat goes on.

A JEWISH WEDDING, JULY 2012

We dress up and put our best foot forward for a birthday, a funeral, or a wedding. They are rendezvous that help us keep faith with our humanity. They are rituals that hold us together, like the glue in a collage.

My son's wedding was no exception. It was impeccably planned and orchestrated. Everyone dressed to the nines. Jews and gentiles came together in peaceful ignorance of each other's traditions, to wish the couple well. I quoted Rabindranath Tagore in my speech and allowed myself to be tossed high on a chair above the heads of the crowd by a bunch of burly lads in dinner suits.

If I had thought I was ignorant of big white weddings, it was nothing compared to my ignorance of the

Jewish version. However, at the end of the two-day celebration, I would be declaring that all weddings should be Jewish and, furthermore, they should all be exactly like my son and his bride's.

PRE-WEDDING EXCITEMENT

A lot happened in the week between our arrival back in Paris after my birthday party in the south and the wedding on Sunday, July 1st.

Ross and Petrea[4] stayed on in the south, visiting places like Marseilles and Saint Raphael. Maxine and her husband, Craig, stayed down south too and visited Avignon, Arles, and Montpellier. Mum flew in from Christchurch and Singapore. Christophe's cousin Emma and her partner, Richie, arrived on the Eurostar from London. It felt like the world was arriving on my doorstep and I spent the week prior to the wedding in a state of high excitement.

Christophe and his bride had been married, according to the law of the Republic, in the town hall of the 15th arrondissement prior to my birthday party. No going up trees or on to beaches to pledge allegiances in France. The church didn't get a piece of the action

---

[4] Ross got married for the third time to Petrea December 27th, 2003

until a mayor representing the secular state of the nation had pronounced the couple legally married. After that, God was welcome and the wedding ceremony could run according to which ever religious form you adhered to. In this case, Jewish.

RENDEZVOUS

During the week before "The Big Day," Mum and I met up with Christophe's dad in a café by the Montparnasse railway station. He was still petulant about our son's marriage. I didn't know if it was because of how much he was having to fork out, or if it was because it was Jewish, or if it was because of his son's choice of bride, or if it was just because he hated anything to do with religious "claptrap." He was left-wing and a fervent supporter of France's secular state. I was too high on anticipation of the event, and so thrilled that my family had come over for it, to feel fazed by his gloom. Mum was really happy to see him again. As far as she was concerned, he was still her son-in-law and the wedding was an excuse to see all the family members she had lost in the divorce.

That's the problem with separation and divorce: It's never just about two people. A whole family structure falls into wrack and ruin and everyone misses out on someone or something. It's hard to maintain contact even with favourite members of one's spouse's family when divorce slices the union in half. There's a lot of fallout. A wedding offers both sides the option of letting bygones be bygones, but that depends on the goodwill of the injured party. At this particular wedding, my ex and I would be walking on either side of our son, up the grassy aisle, between the guests, to the chuppah. I didn't know how it would be on the actual day but with luck, enough time had passed since our divorce in 1996 for us to be of good cheer on July 1st.

The meeting in the café was a gesture in this direction. It went really well.

"I'm wearing a Nehru-styled Indian jacket," he announced as if defying some sort of imposed dress code.

"I'm wearing Punjabi trousers with a silk Kurta." I chuckled. "We'll look like a couple of old baba-cools."

We were both delighted to have hit on an Indian theme for a Jewish wedding. It was a wink to our hippie days, thirty years back, when we had first met on a bus off the east coast of Africa.

The café rendezvous had taken place in the middle of the week. At the end of the week, June 29th, the rest of the family arrived back in Paris. We gathered inside Le Train Bleu, a gorgeous Belle Epoque restaurant overlooking the railway lines of the Gare de Lyon. The gilded flamboyant décor of its interior surpassed the quality of the food which was, in turn, surpassed by the price. Being together with my family in Paris was priceless and surpassed all else. In short, I was happy.

THE SYNAGOGUE

The following morning, the men donned skullcaps and we all shuffled into the back row of Rabbi Tom's synagogue in the 17th arrondissement. I had been in historical synagogues in The Netherlands and Spain so was surprised to find myself in the lounge of someone's apartment. Admittedly, it had been stripped of everything that could identify it as a lounge, but there was no mistaking that it had once been someone's living quarters. There were fold-up metal chairs arranged in rows across the "lounge" and there was a dais at the front of the room. There was a little cabinet covered with a blue velvet curtain behind the dais. I had imagined something a bit more churchlike: pews and pictures, no crosses obviously, "straightness" softened by a few flowers. I picked up what I took to be a Bible and discovered that not only was it upside down but also back to front. I wanted to giggle but didn't dare. I was "in church." I snuck a peek at the rest of the family and saw that they, too, were looking bamboozled. I peered over the shoulder of the person seated in front of me, looking for clues. My Bro' just asked his neighbour outright, "How does this work?" I didn't know what kind of religious upbringing my brother had had. I had never asked him directly but had gleaned that both his "parents" had been staunch Prods. He took the synagogue in his stride. Nothing ever seemed to faze him.

I left the converted apartment feeling intelligent and included in the liberal community my son had chosen to join. I had done seven years of scripture exams, by choice, during my childhood. I had loved the Bible stories from both testaments. So, while the structure of the service and the implements of worship had been different, I had felt at home—relatively speaking. When Christophe had been called forward to read from the Torah, it had been by his Jewish name. That had rung strangely in my ears, until I remembered that I, too, sported a foreign name, given to me by my own spiritual teacher. My name was Yashoda—adoptive mother of the baby Krishna. Swami Veetamohananda, then the president of the Ramakrishna Mission in France, had given it to me around the time I met my brother. I don't remember if it was before or after our meeting and I have never thought to analyse the significance of the role Yashoda plays in Indian mythology and the role adoption has played in my own family story.[5]

I had booked massages for the "girls" on the Saturday afternoon and a hairdresser for Sunday morning at home. It felt odd to be going to a wedding on a Sunday and even more odd to have my hair done, sitting outside, at home on a Sunday morning. I had discovered that some hairdressers were happy to make a bit of extra cash by catering to these Sunday ceremonies. I offered her five heads for tarting up. Everyone got their money's worth.

We set off in two cars for the Normandy countryside, just after lunch on July 1st. We dropped our gear at the B&B, dressed in our finery, did due diligence on our appearance, met with mutual approval, and then drove a further fifteen minutes to the farmhouse. We were ready for the late-afternoon ceremony. My only child was getting married.

THE WEDDING CEREMONY

A Jewish marriage canopy stood white and sturdy at one end of the farmhouse lawn. Chairs, covered in white cloth, were arranged in rows on either side of an emerald aisle.

---

[5] Please see my first book, *Once a Pilgrim, Always a Coach*, if you are interested in reading the indepth journey of my spiritual growth.

Looking back on the photos, I am critical not only of my attire, but also of the sunglasses that I have not removed. I look like I might have been crying, playing at film stars, or hiding a black eye. I was the only one wearing sunglasses even though the waning sun was still bright enough to merit them. Was I the object of whispered stories about the mother of the groom—the mother-in-law? I didn't see myself in these roles and still less in the fairytale equivalent of the stepmother. The French only have one word for both stepmother and mother-in-law: belle mère. The irony was in the translation of the word "belle" meaning beautiful. I didn't think I looked particularly beautiful that day, but then I was almost officially sixty years old. I was a stepmother to Richard's two adult children. Decidedly older women don't fare well in fairytales and this was a fairytale wedding. Whatever role I was playing in the story, the simple fact of the matter was, I forgot to change my sunglasses for my clear ones. I didn't want a fuzzy version of this major event in my life and my sunglasses served two purposes: seeing and shading. My ex and I walked our son to the chuppah and I wore sunglasses.

I don't remember what was said, but it all made sense: a tent with open sides, a marriage contract, rings exchanged, a glass broken, shouts of joy, a fiddler and circle dancing. It was a summer song, a poem in white lace. And all the people who mattered to me were there to share it. I felt blessed.

THE PARTY

The religious ceremony over, the crowd moved towards the cocktail venue. The fiddler kept fiddling while the guests mingled, holding aperitifs and snacking on pre-dinner delicacies. The photographs were taken on the lawn before the sun was too low to be helpful and before we were herded into the transformed barn for the wedding reception. My ex was at a table with all his family and I was at another table with all my family. I introduced my brother and his wife to my ex-in-laws and Mum chatted to them as if I had never left their family. I picked up where we had left off some twenty years earlier with one of my former sisters-in-law and her German husband. The band hit the opening number and bride and groom strode into their party to a fanfare of whoops and swirling white table napkins. All the months of organising and agonising over the organising paid off. They enjoyed their own party! Seeing them enjoying themselves gave everyone else permission to let their hair down.

And we did! We pounded the floor to "Hava Nagila" in a circle that spun perilously faster and faster, spitting out the weak and holding the fit in a tight embrace. We spun around the bridal couple hoisted high above our heads on chairs held firmly by their friends. My son's wife was petite, but he had the build of a rugby forward. I watched their friends bouncing them both and muttered a short prayer for a soft landing or the availability of a good medical service. And then I had my turn up there. When in Rome! I didn't know who was the craziest: the lads who tossed me around or me trying to copy the couple and her parents by raising one arm above my head while being bounced. Champagne helped! Sweat poured off me. I had made a brilliant choice of Punjabi attire for dancing and chair tossing. I wondered if Christophe had made his choice of groomsmen based on their athletic ability. At one moment deep into the night, one of them threw himself onto the ground in the middle of the dance floor and another leapt over him and lay alongside him—and then another—and another—until there were no more groomsmen left to leap. And then it was "open bar." There were six on the floor, face up, the music was wild, the crowd gathered round, screaming encouragement. I saw Richie, Ross's future son-in-law, leap into the fray and soar over the top of the previous six and throw himself onto the floor making, it seven in a row. It was Christophe's turn—rite of passage as the groom? I no longer knew what was part of a Jewish wedding ritual and what was a twenty-first-century version of a bunch of lads throwing down the gauntlet.

There was the anticipated chocolate fountain and macaroon mountain. There was a softly sung poem of love in Hebrew about the night and roses. There were speeches that teased and praised; videos that revealed as well as honoured friendship; music and dancing—and more dancing—and still more dancing.

The following morning, my body told me it had covered the mountain stretch of the Tour de France the night before, and that it did not want to get back in the saddle for a few more days. When the other members of the family emerged late morning, they looked like they had been on the same cycling team as me. We drove back to the venue for an afters event, which was mostly about sharing a brunch with bleary-eyed wedding guests. It felt like a Monday morning, except no one was going to work.

That Monday afternoon has slid from memory, as has the rest of the week. The summer of 2012 meandered on. I bathed in the joy and happiness I had been granted. I said goodbye to my brother and his wife, to my sister and her husband, to my mother.

And the beat goes on.

Questions

Can you spot any patterns in your family of origin? Anything that seems to be repeating itself in your current family system? What impact, if any, does it have on your own life?

Which members of your family do you connect the most with? Why?

Which members of your family don't you fit in with? Why not?

Which Christmas do you remember the most? What makes it memorable?

Where were you at the turn of the century? Who were you with? What do you remember about the event?

On a scale of 1 to 10, how do you rank yourself as being open to other cultures and religions?

What is one birthday or wedding you remember with great happiness? With intense regret or sadness?

PART THREE

Party's Over

THE WHATSAPP DIALOGUES

– SEPTEMBER TO NOVEMBER 2021

SEPTEMBER 20ᵀᴴ

Ross tries to reach me on WhatsApp. I see it's him but am working online, doing coaching with a group. I send him a quick message: "Bro', I am teaching today and tomorrow—I'll try calling you during the week—early morning or night time for me—Hugs."

"OK, I need five minutes of your time—about me. Shall I send you a message then we can talk?"

"I can call you just after 13h my time—11pm your time," I ping back. I immediately send a further message, "Yes, send me your question with a wee bit of context before we talk."

"It's about my health. Can you call me after 11pm?"

He signs his messages to me with XXs. I send smileys with hearts.

"OK, Bro, will do."

I call him during the break and he gives me his news. His words land in me like a foot stepping onto an undetected landmine.

"You remember that lump I had removed from my back thirteen years ago?"

"Yeah, I remember. It had been one of those suspect things that hadn't been behaving like a healthy cell was supposed to."

"Well, I had a bowel screen a wee while back and it turned out to be positive. I've been having a few aches and pains in different parts of my body and the doc had me do some X-rays and a CT scan."

I'm not taking a lot of air into my lungs. There's a tightening at the back of my neck.

"I've got secondary cancers in various parts of my body. I've got a few more tests to do to locate the primary source. We're starting with a liver biopsy. Anyway, going forward, surgery is not an option but chemo, radiation, drugs are all on the cards. So, all good!"

He's back in his old job as a radio broadcaster. He's announcing the local weather forecast. It won't rain tomorrow. All good.

"Anyway, how are you, Sis?"

"Fine, fine."

I've just lost both legs in the explosion, but I'm fine. There's no time left to chat. I have to be back online with my group in three minutes. I tell him I'll call as soon as I can.

"Lovely to talk, Sis."

We click out.

I send the group off into breakout rooms almost immediately. I cut my mic and camera and hit Google search. I go for frequently asked questions about cancer. I discover things about primary and secondary tumours that I don't want to learn. There is a strong possibility that my beloved brother is, barring miracles, a condemned man.

I whip a quick message back to him, dressing my shock in a garment to please and humour.

"No half measures with you, Bro'! I'd tell you to pull your hair out and scream but then remembered you didn't have any left to pull!! Full steam ahead, Bro'—I'm behind you all the way!"

He knows he has my love and support, even across the 19,000+ kilometres, as the crow flies, that separate where I am from where he is.

"Don't hesitate to call me!"

"Thanks, Sis, you're a tower of strength. I've spoken to Mum. Not sure how she took it. I think she's getting secondary and primary mixed up. I'm in Wanaka this weekend, so I've arranged to see her around 1h30 pm on Sunday. I'm feeling good today."

I don't feel like a "tower of strength." Between feeling annoyed and helpless, I accuse them both of avoiding reality. *Why is his mother, our mother, confused about what is primary and what is secondary?* I want her to be a tower of strength! I want her to reassure him—to tell him it will be alright. I want magic! My "happy families" dream pops to the surface again and rubs against me like wet sand inside a dry bathing suit.

I remember a few years back when, walking along South Brighton Beach with Mum, she began telling me about my father's shortcomings. She may well have done this many times before, but I had always been willing to see him through her eyes. I agreed without saying that Dad was a negative kind of guy. He said "no" before he said "yes" to any suggestion coming from her. An argument would ensue, leaving me feeling helpless between them—not that my help was ever sought or needed.

This time, however, and after a few years of therapy, I rebuffed her.

"He's your husband, but he is my father. It's not the same. We don't see him the same way."

I sounded tetchy. I wanted to reclaim him as the guy who balanced me, side saddle, on his bicycle bar to go down to Brighton Beach before he owned a car; the guy who took me out into the big surf in my stretchy red bubble bathing suit and dug holes in the sand with me; the guy who built me a dolls' house on the back lawn. He never said much to me that I remember but I liked mucking around in the garden with him. We lived in a cold, monosyllabic house. Looking back on the child that I was, I see someone who grew up between a very handsome man and a beautiful, vivacious woman, neither of whom were heard speaking to each other in her company. "Children should be seen and not heard" was an adage often quoted at the table by her father. The child that I was, believed him. Down at the beach, tumbled in sea and rolled in sand, words were extraneous; happiness easy. My parents were a dazzling couple in the company of others. They attracted laughter and dancing. The little girl I remember, did everything she could to shine in her mother's eyes, but it was impossible to replace something her mother had lost and could not talk about.

We often went to my nana's for Saturday night tea or Sunday lunch. Hers was a warm, garrulous house. Mum, Dad, my sister, and I all loved her. She said things like, "The Queen is such a lovely lady, but I wouldn't want her job." She was married to a man called Bas who took me on his milk rounds when I was small. I rode beside him in a van with a sliding door and waited on the bench seat while he delivered milk in glass quart and pint bottles to the front doorstep of all the houses on his route. Sometimes he let me carry the empty bottles back to his van, where I put them into crates on the floor at the back. The quart bottles were large in my little hands, but I never let one drop. I felt important and proud of my helpfulness. He painted houses and worked in a bread factory too, but I never helped him on either of those jobs.

Nana baked fruitcake and made sweet milky cups of tea when we went to their house. Sometimes Mum, Dad, Nana, and Bas all sat around a square fold-up table covered in green felt and played cards. On winter Sunday afternoons or cold Saturday nights, a fire roared in the hearth. Dad and Nana swapped yarns and ate cake. Mum shared the jokes but not the sugar.

Mum had grown up without a father. He had died of lung cancer when she was only eighteen months old. She didn't like her stepfather, Bas, whom she had been introduced to on the day her mother married him. She was twelve at the time. The hurt and disappointment she had felt when her mother brought a foreign man into the house lay buried beneath her bones. Her and my father's forty-three-year moratorium on all reference to their son shoved shame and anger into that same pit of loneliness. They would lie alongside each other, unattended, for the rest of her life.

Many years later when we had that conversation walking along South Brighton Beach, I wasn't blaming her for criticizing her husband. I just wanted my father to stand in my own eyes and not in her hurt. The words, "He's your husband, but he's my father" were true but my tone of voice betrayed the accusation. The words judged as only a child can judge a parent for perceived failures. She said nothing further. Anything she felt plunged into the graveyard far below the surface to lie beside all the other wounds.

So, when Ross called her to say primary and secondary cancers had been located in various parts of his body, she was programmed not to have words available for any feelings she may have had. She was, indeed, confused.

My brother has inherited her skill of blocking unpleasant emotions and, seen from the outside, their shared capacity to focus on the "positive" is their mutual "tower of strength."

There is something horribly undeniable about the power of computerised tomography to show you what is. How can you look at a scan that shows your insides riddled with cancerous tumours and remain positive? But he is! It's possible that, even though he has an amazing capacity to always look on the bright side of life, his current super- positive attitude is more like a phase two emotional reaction to life-changing news: denial. Phase one is shock and that's where I am.

Now is not the time to give him a lesson on Kübler-Ross's work[6] or to try any unsolicited coaching. I want to shake him out of his ultra-positive attitude, so we can have a "real" conversation. I don't know what he thinks or feels. Does he know his goose is cooked but is just pretending it isn't?

Maybe this super-positive person is really "him" and I just can't believe it myself. He didn't inherit that trait from his biological father, so where does it come from? Has he been like this all his life? How would I know?

I want to know why this has happened. The unanswerable questions fill my mind like sand castles standing sure of themselves whilst the tide is out. *What has caused all these tumours to sprout like mushrooms in the dark moist soil of his insides?* I read there is a correlation between repressed rage and the onset of cancer. Is my brother raging, silently, beneath his beaming smile? Does he keep it at bay by constant movement to the next project, the next acquisition, the next problem to solve? If anger is there, I could share some of it myself, in the form of disappointment that so much time has dribbled away without ever having

---

[6] In her book *On Death and Dying*, Elizabeth Kübler-Ross depicts five stages of grief. A later model "the change curve" adds "shock" as a first reaction to loss.

had the conversations that count—at least, for me. I do want to know how it really was for him growing up as an adopted, albeit much-loved, child. *How did he handle the unconscious debt?* He did tell me once that he had been hurt when an aunt had left him an unequal share of her inheritance because he wasn't a bona fide heir, coming from "foreign" loins. I remember him also saying, years ago, that he had sometimes wished his parents had been younger. I didn't tell him that I got them young and beautiful, but before they were old enough to forgive each other.

My shoulders sag, and my jaw slackens, realizing quite clearly that nothing can be different from what it is. This is what the story is. I think glumly that even if I were there with him now, I would be useless as a caregiver. I avoided sickness like the plague. Mum, Ross, and I all prided ourselves on our robust health. In fact, we flaunted it. My mother, in particular, took good care of her diet, did regular exercise, and avoided pharmaceutical solutions. Ross was a sugar binger but also an exercise freak. He did paracetamol for anything painful. I met them midway on all three manias.

I don't share many of these thoughts and certainly not my feelings with either of them. Not even during my regular Sunday-morning call to Mum.

"Have you heard from Ross?"

"Yes, he's going to pop in for a coffee next Sunday."

"I suppose he gave you his news?" I feel apprehensive about broaching the subject and don't know why. I may be afraid of the intense sorrow that is lurking in the shadows. Or I may be afraid of the rage that is sorrow's playmate.

"Yes, he said he had cancer."

"He told me you were a wee bit confused between what was a primary and what was a secondary tumour."

"Not at all! I've had cancer too, you know. I know what it's like." She is adamant and I don't feel I can go any further without one of my "playmates" taking over the conversation, so I change it. It is something the three of us have in common: the ability to avoid the unpleasant, the annoying, the devastating. It's all part of the "think positive" syndrome we adhere to religiously—in public—and between ourselves.

SEPTEMBER 22ND

Ross sends a screenshot of an app, showing weight gain and loss. It shows weight gain.

"And here's me thinking you were resorting to stage four cancer to LOSE weight, Bro. Silly me!"

Despite the small increase, it still indicates just how much weight he has actually lost.

"Try reducing your sugar intake—less painful!"

"Love your approach, Sis, but it's alcohol that's going to do it for me."

I hope he means he's cut down on—or out—on the alcohol. We bat a few more silly messages back and forth until he writes, "On a serious note—just for a mo', I don't now need a liver biopsy, so I go straight on to Keytruda by infusion—about every three weeks. The polyp under my tongue was a melanoma hence the change in approach. My melanoma from thirteen years ago was the primary source, so, oncology treatment soon to get sorted out."

I read the last lines a few times over, incredulous at first, that he needs to apologise for being "serious for a moment." I recall one of the jokes circulating through cyberspace during the COVID lockdown in 2020: "Life is too serious to take seriously." I recognise then that Ross and I have an unspoken agreement that banter is best. We are loyal to our kinsfolk and our British colonial heritage when we under-speak our pain.

Thinking about his weight report takes me back to the time when we both went on diets. We egged each other on with weekly weight check-ins. I religiously logged my achievements in a little green book. We were his motto "Set the Goal—Get the Goal" incarnate! We kept up the competition for three months and at the end of it, I had lost two jean sizes and he, ten kilos. It was fun and it was easy. I showed up in New Zealand for Christmas of that year looking very svelte. Even my mother said that my new weight suited me. She hated the big-boned, fat-arsed build of the women in Dad's family. She liked the thinness I wore in my younger years. I was willowy, graceful, athletic, and clothes hung easily over skin and bone. Looking at me that Christmas, she saw a self that belonged on her side of the family, and that pleased her. While her praise was a reward for my efforts, it didn't bode well for my future approval ratings as my body continued to age. Then, though, I just enjoyed the way I looked in her eyes.

Had my brother, unconsciously, sought approval in her eyes too? I don't know and it's not something I'm ever likely to be able to ask him now.

SEPTEMBER 24ᵀᴴ

I Google "Keytruda treatment" and find a PDF document to send to him that explains how to track cancer symptoms. I want to feel helpful, so I ignore the likelihood that he will have already done his own research.

"This doc might feed your conversation with the oncologist, Bro'. Keytruda treatment costs an absolute fortune! I wouldn't be immune to making some of that lovely lolly!! Hope you've got a good insurance policy, Bro'!"

He comes back with "It's now free in New Zealand." He doesn't mention insurance. "I got a letter today saying I can't get into see an oncologist for four to six weeks. Bugger! I'm seeing my doctor on Monday. I'm going to try consulting a private physician—will let you know."

I deliberately do not pursue my half-joking question about insurance but hope he's got full coverage.

A second message arrives on a different note. "Got some good news tonight! Got an agreement between the vendor and the purchaser on price for the property I am selling in Ote. So, a good end to the day."

He can't see an oncologist for weeks, but the treatment is free! He's just qualified as a real estate agent in record time and is selling a house. He's over the moon about it, but he could be dead before the sale goes through!

This is absurd!

His boat still has its keel in place, but mine has lost the wind from its sail and is in danger of keeling over. I don't recognize the country I grew up in.

The country I grew up in gave me a university education and a good set of teeth—things my parents could not have afforded on their modest incomes at the time.

I got holiday jobs, like most students, to pay for books and incidental tuition fees. Subsidised higher education gave access to universities, provided you passed the entrance exam. I never had to resort to bank loans and insurance policies to be able to see a doctor or a specialist in the New Zealand I grew up in. I grew up in a country of progressive social thinking. It was the first country in the world to give women the vote (in 1893!). It was one of the first to introduce oldage pensions and state housing.

The country I grew up in has given me beautiful teeth and a university degree but it won't give my brother an appointment to see an oncologist today. I don't get it and no one I speak to in the family can explain it either.

It's only been five days since the news of his health hurtled towards me with all the speed and power of a curveball. I'm still standing despite its force. It hasn't travelled in slow motion, cartoon-like, down the table as it did on that birthday night twenty-seven years ago. Then, I was saying hello to him and my heart knew the colour and warmth of a summer sun. Now, it seems I must say goodbye to him and my heart feels the cold grey tones of an approaching European winter.

I'd rather sell a house too, than feel like my life is about to be ripped from under my feet. Doing anything at all is better than waiting to see an oncologist who could save your life, but who is not available at the moment to do that.

I generally avoid consulting doctors. They scare me. However, I feel spooked enough by what's happening to him to make an appointment to see a skin specialist.

I have consulted at least six dermatologists since deciding to live in France over forty years ago. I have disliked all of them. They have all been women and they have talked down to me in their meticulous medical language. They have all made me feel small and unintelligent and I have invariably sulked and refused to eat my vegetables. When I really was a child, my mother would admonish me for my selfishness. "Think of all the starving children in India who don't have vegetables to eat." Faced with powerful professional women doctors who spoke a language I could not understand, I shrunk easily back to my five-year-old self. I wanted to poke my tongue out and say in a cheeky voice, "So, wrap them up and send them to India!"

Seated across a consulting table from a French dermatologist, I tended to glare, say little, and expect her to guess what the problem was.

When I make the appointment to see a seventh dermatologist, I decide that, under the circumstances, I must remain age sixty-nine and one metre eighty tall, whether sitting or prostrate on the examination table.

My skin is covered with a mass of brown spots of varying sizes. Any one of those spots could be keeping a nasty secret. I might be pre-disposed towards cancer. Cancer runs in the family. Nana died of skin cancer. A long time ago, I had a sun spot removed surgically from my inner thigh because it was diagnosed as having cells that were dividing unconventionally. It was removed from the exact same part of the leg that Nana's cancer had started from. That piece of news dumped a bucket load of butterflies in my belly. My mother had a cancerous tumour removed from her bowel in 2018. Unlike my brother, twenty years her junior, she moved fluidly through the system from doctor to surgeon to operating table and back home again. *Why is it so different with Ross? Is it incurable? Is he beyond hope already? Why don't we know? And has he got butterflies as well as tumours in his belly? And how is his wife dealing with this? How are his kids taking this information on board?* I don't actually pick up the phone to ask. I want to continue denying that it is happening. I care but can't share. That would make it real.

I tell myself that it can't be all bad though because he's selling a house. I have implicitly agreed that this "thing" can be kicked, through grit and willpower. It's a question of attitude. I want him to sell many more houses.

And then someone reminds me of the adage "Man

plans, and God laughs."

I don't want Her to laugh at my brother's plans to sell houses and go places. I want Her to help us play "Let's Pretend." Someone I love is dying and I want Her to save him.

Please.

While God is laughing, my brother and I tacitly agree that all is well and improving by the minute.

SEPTEMBER 25TH

I send him a flier about a new master class in coaching I'm going to run in the UK. We're both show-offs and that's what I am doing by sending him this flier. But what I'm really doing is saying, "Talk to me, Bro'—tell me what you think—tell me you are still there."

I used to enjoy discussing some of my business concerns with him. His experience in the boardroom was something I didn't have and I valued his opinion. I never thought to ask my dad anything like that; I just assumed he had nothing to say. Having a brother who loves to be consulted and has lots of experience and knowledge to share... this has been twenty-seven years in the making. I don't want our chats to end.

He doesn't respond.

When Dad was dying back in 2010 and before we

could say that word out loud, my mother called me in Paris on a Wednesday in March.

"Your dad is in hospital."

"Is this it, then?"

"I think so."

The Singapore Airlines ticketing agency recognised the urgency and got me on a flight the following day but couldn't book me for a return on the Sunday eleven days later. I agreed to come back the day before.

I was standing in a queue at Charles de Gaulle, waiting to check in. A sales assistant was moving down the line checking that all was well with his business-class passengers. Such solicitous behaviour was unexpected, albeit agreeable. When he got to me, I looked at him and asked without much hope, "I don't suppose you could change my return from Saturday to Sunday, by any chance?"

I held my breath as he interrupted his colleague at the counter and hunched over her computer. He came back with a smile and a return ticket for the Sunday.

God might have been laughing but She was also planning!

I touched down in Christchurch at ten on Saturday morning after two long flights to the other side of the world.

Dad was moved from his bed in a Christchurch

public hospital to a room in a hospice on the Tuesday. Did he know he was dying? Did we know he was dying? There seemed to be a silent agreement between Mum, Dad, my sister, and myself to know, without ever actually saying, that, yes, he was dying.

The weather that last week of March was an autumnal palette of blue: sharp in the morning, periwinkle in the afternoon, and ink in the evening. We walked the beaches in the mornings, visited the hospice in the afternoons, and played Scrabble in the evenings.

The hospice doubled as a home for dementia patients. I saw them all sitting in a circle in comfy chairs in the lounge area whenever I walked in. I had to walk past them to reach the corridor that took me to Dad's private room. I faked a smile and waved a greeting whilst moving swiftly past them. I didn't want to linger in the company of their vacant, lopsided faces and flaccid bodies. I felt like I was walking into the lobby of the Hotel California, seeing people who had checked out but who had a long wait before leaving. That thought made my gut squirm. It was a relief to get to Dad's room, to spend time with him before he checked out.

A strange thing happened on the Tuesday of that week. It was on the day that Dad was transferred from the public hospital to the hospice and it wasn't the first time that something similar had happened to me. My entire right leg had locked one morning on my pilgrimage to the tomb of Saint James in Santiago, Spain. This time it was just the right ankle that seized up and transformed my usual gait from a determined thrust forward to a hesitant hobble. I had sat down in an armchair in Dad's "new" room to admire what Maxine had done to make the room more homey: paintings on the wall and photos on the bedside table. I had chatted about nothing in particular to Dad and when it came time to leave, I had swung myself up to standing position and promptly collapsed back into the chair with a gasp of pain. There was no logical explanation for the bone jam and I had no intention of wasting precious time consulting someone about it, so I accepted "the message" to change gears for a week.

If the weather was a palette of blue, my moods were a palette of red. My mother began decluttering the house of Dad's presence. She emptied Dad's clothes into plastic bags and stacked his garage tools into cardboard boxes. It was her way of dealing with his imminent demise, but I turned chili red watching it. Words churned and seethed inside me, like clothes in an old-fashion washing machine. They had to be put through the wringer to squeeze out excess venom before they could be hung up outside.

"He's not effing dead yet!" I wanted to scream at

her but instead turned my back and went out into the garden until my mood cooled to watermelon.

On the Friday, a nurse came to tell us that they would be putting Dad on a morphine pump that night. She warned us that we would no longer be able to communicate with him. I didn't fully understand then, that this was how the medical profession dealt, as kindly as it could, with an elderly patient whose time had come. He was about to enter a land from which he would not return and it was time to say our final goodbyes. Even so, it was not possible to predict how long he would cling on to life and the medical staff were not offering to hasten his decision. Or was God involved again?

Driving to the hospice on my own the following morning, I spoke loudly and clearly to God so She could hear me as plain as day. "I am leaving tomorrow. Please come for him before I go!" It was more of an order than a plea, but I had absolute faith in the ears that would hear me. Certainty resonated in every cell of my body.

His bed had been turned towards the window two days earlier. It mirrored a psychic experience I had had during a facilitated exercise with a friend back in Paris just a week prior to Mum's call and my subsequent return home. In that experience, I had struggled with not knowing whether I had the power to open both the real window as well as the symbolic one.

I was none the wiser when I sat down beside his bed that Saturday morning.

I spoke with quiet lucidity, as if I knew what I was talking about. "We are here. We love you. I love you. No one can go through the door with you. You have to do this one on your own, Dad. And, you can go whenever it seems most right to you. Just know I am leaving tomorrow at midday." I said this gently and with great clarity of mind—as if there could be no doubt as to the truth of my words.

I had only just gone to bed that night when I heard the phone ring a little after ten. I felt a curious mixture of excitement and relief as I dressed hurriedly. He had "taken off" before me. I felt blessed and anxious to get back to the hospice as fast as possible.

All three of us took turns to sit alone with him in his room. The window, which I had not opened, was slightly ajar. The air in the room was filled with a sharp scent of early autumn. His presence was still tangible but no longer confined to his body. I received this moment as the Divine extending a great and kindly hand towards those of us remaining on this side of the door.

And I still left later that morning, as planned. I was grateful for a single seat with its private window, so I could cry quietly as the plane made its slow taxi down the runway. As the engines went into full throttle for takeoff, I gave full vent to anguished sobbing. Through blurry eyes, I saw the land of sheep and fields; rivers and farmland diminishing rapidly beneath and the Southern Alps looming ahead in stately dignity. It takes just twenty minutes to fly east to west, and be torn from one's roots and swallowed up in sky and the Tasman Sea. When my hand steadied and the land was no longer visible, I began my last of the very few letters I had written to my Dad during his life time. I would send it in email form from Singapore and my brother would read it out at his funeral a few days later.

When Ross dies, I know I will not be there for his funeral service either. I don't even have an airline ticket this time. Even if I got to the border, I would be refused entry. The country is closed. It's in lockdown.

My grief waits in the wings, preparing her lines. The other part of me, though, continues to send messages via WhatsApp. He supplements the brevity of his replies with photos or videos of daily life with friends and family. His wife Petrea feeds the blog they have created for their many friends and colleagues with news of his health.

OCTOBER

For the first two weeks of the month, we continue the charade of business-as-usual. When we exchange photos of our respective grandchildren, we joke about how fast they are all growing and how time is running away from us.

Not running away, just out. There is no need to say it.

He tells me in one message how impressed he is that friends have been over to stay and have mowed the lawns for him. I see his WOW smiley and realize that this is something new for him. He's used to being the one to help. The old saying "What goes around comes around" does not mean something negative in this case, but rather a positive cycle of give and get. I feel chuffed that he's so pleased.

He also mentions that he is still waiting to hear from an oncologist. "Patience is not my thing." He LOLs.

"No shit—must run in the family," I ping back.

He sends me a video of a TV report on the devastating fires in Ohau the previous year. He wants me to see him on TV, in his role of newly elected councilman, representing the mayor of the Waitaki District Council. He is proud of the way he was there, on the spot, in the minute, handling the situation with aplomb and care. I see him in his full authority, doing what he does best: holding centre stage with legitimacy.

"How're y' doin', Bro'?"

"Pretty good actually—sore back but managing with paracetamol," he replies.

He writes more but it comes with a lot of typos. He realizes it and sends a second message through.

"Hells bells! Apologies for my text above—spelling/fingers and ME not checking."

I take this as a good sign, even though I'm guessing that the tumour growing on his brain is, in fact, the most likely culprit.

It's still October when he responds to one of my regular enquiries into the state of his health.

"Hi, Sis. Good actually. May get into see another oncologist earlier than expected but waiting to hear. Trying for a private consultation first, before I go to the public oncologist. Paracetamol and tramadol are the pain relievers. Managing the pain well. Had some more blood tests but haven't had the analysis of these back yet. So overall pretty good. Lost a little bit more weight so hovering around 96.2kgs. I was 100.2 kgs on September 6th so lost 4 kgs. Mentally very strong and physically OK—just hard to bend over and lift stuff, so I ask for help. Sold another house."

"Hey, you're getting good at this! House selling, I mean, not pain killers!"

I get LOLs in return and an update on his absence of treatment.

"Had a good call this morning with oncology at public hospital. After my appointment on Monday, October 25th, he will prepare treatment plan and that will go straight to hospital. So, I don't then have to see another oncologist. Yea! They told me I've shortcut the system by between two to four weeks. So, very happy with that."

I don't remind him that it has taken five weeks for him to get to even talk to an oncologist. He finally has a concrete action plan and that brings him relief.

I make a stab at optimism, "Good for you, Bro'."

Shortly after this exchange, I send a message asking if I can give him a call. I'd just like to hear his voice and am taking a few days' break away from Paris, so I have flexible hours.

He replies immediately, saying that he'd like that too, but he is about to go into a meeting, so could I call before or after that. He attaches a weight chart with the comment "rapid reduction over a month."

He gets one of my cute observations in return: "Yeah, and I bet it's not due to eating lettuce every day!"

His LOLs come back with "Trying to stabilize in the 93 kgs range."

OCTOBER 16ᵀᴴ

He writes that he is about to drive home from a party in Oamaru. His message is brief and not completely comprehensible. The abbreviations are not completely recognizable as text speak.

He's about to drive a car home!!! It's only an hour's drive from Oamaru to Ote where he lives, but still....

I don't know what to think. It's just less than a month since he told me he has stage four cancer, that he still hasn't seen an oncologist, that he is treating the pain with paracetamol. If he is driving around the countryside and going to meetings and parties, maybe there are different degrees of stage four cancers. Maybe his is a mild version—the annoying kind—the type that doesn't ever go away but just hangs around being a nuisance. I want to believe that.

Two days later, his wife sends a photo of him in his dressing gown, sitting beside the outdoor spa. He has lost a lot of weight and his smile is awkward. It's not the booming, beaming brother who radiates energy out into any space he walks into, sitting there looking at the camera. His picture puts paid to magical thinking.

OCTOBER 25TH

Petrea drives him to Dunedin Public Hospital where they meet up with James, his forty-one-year old son who has driven up from Invercargill. They have a consultation with a specialist. It is Labour Day in New Zealand and NO ONE works that day. I realize what this visit must be costing. He doesn't tell me about the outcome of the trip. I don't consult the blog. It's efficient but not for me. I haven't fully embraced social media like he has and excuse my deficiency by telling myself that I don't want to share my brother's demise in the public domain.

OCTOBER 30TH

"Hi, Sis, I am about to be appointed to a new governance role on Well South in a couple of weeks. Quite excited! This means I won't be standing for Council in October next year."

He sounds buoyant, almost exuberant.

"Well done! Bro'," is my immediate response. My brother, who is most surely dying, has been appointed to a board called "Well South." Wanting to match his excitement but also note the irony in the name of the company, I add, "The Universe is laughing with you. It is all part of the 'Think-Positive' strategy that won't fail you—I love it!"

And because he always has to have the last say, he comes back with "Off to sleep now."

I hope he sleeps while God is laughing.

God must be the Joker in the Universe who wants us to feel the lightness of being in the gravity of our existence. My brother is going to leave us all whilst everything is inviting him to stay longer: more boards to belong to; more properties to sell; more community activism to engage in as a councilman; more family, friends, and colleagues to entertain with his bigger-than-big smile.

NOVEMBER 8TH

"Hi, Bro'—decided to write rather than try calling again. I am understanding that the little energy available to you right now is being mobilised for just getting through each day as it comes. I understand that you are maintaining a 'business as usual' approach to every day, but even to do that, you need a lot of recoup time. I don't want to add to that by creating a necessity for you to talk to me. I know you are not well at all but that it is important for you to 'carry on'—to 'just-get-on-with-it.' I agree with the strategy, Bro'. I just want to tell you that I love you—that you have been the greatest gift in my life—that I am here in absentia for talking but, of course, useless as a care giver. As soon as Jacinda[7] opens up shop, I am on a plane, but she is not too keen for the moment. Your kids love you. Potroa loves you. Your grandkids love you. Your two sisters love you. God willing, all will be well—you will be well—all is as it should be. Much love Bro'. Sis."

"Hi, Sis, that's very nice, very caring and thank you for being there and supporting me. Love you heaps as well." He signs off with five more kisses than usual.

I feel pushed for time. I have to say things that I absolutely want him to hear, before it is too late. I feel the coming loss and I am far away, miserable, and helpless.

NOVEMBER 12TH

We share what turns out to be our last exchange of texts.

"Have a good day, today, Bro'. I'm off to bed. It's getting chilly here now so bed is the warmest option right now. How's business?" It's a futile, albeit hopeful, question.

He responds saying he's going into a Keytruda call at ten. He says it's about preparation for a first session the following Monday in Dunedin. After the call, he

---

[7] Jacinda Adern, Prime Minister of New Zealand from 2017 to 2023

comes back with more information. He is still his bright cheerful self, albeit, a thinner one.

"On Monday morning, we head off to get planning done with radiation planning on my back, then another CT scan after that—all in Dunedin at Oncology. So, it's all Keytruda after that. This coming week I have James and Emma coming to stay for the week. Be very busy. Now weighing 86 kilos I am down from 102 on September 2nd. OK. Have a good read and go to sleep. HA! HA! Love you Sis, from me."

I retort kindly that we are shortly going weigh the same amount. As hoped for, he doesn't leave me with the last word and I get more kisses back. These small loving signs are indeed his final legacy to me.

I don't realise this. I just feel relieved that something is finally happening. It all sounds so positive that I am willing to believe salvation is on its way. I truly want to believe that action will bring with it a cure—at least more than paracetamol is likely to! I do feel hopeful. Despite this overwhelmingly delightful piece of thinking, the professional in me still hears the denial phase on Elizabeth Kübler-Ross's curve. It's a lovely cosy warm place, like my bed, and I absolutely want to stay there for as long as I can.

NOVEMBER 14ᵀᴴ (SUNDAY)

I send him a short message to wish him luck on the morrow.

"Hang in there! This is the big one, so give it your best shot, Bro!'"

NOVEMBER 15ᵀᴴ (MONDAY)

Petrea drives him to Dunedin Public, where he is given pre-treatment for the radiation planned for the next day. He is back home in Ote that night, where his two adult kids are waiting for him. They drive him the two and a half hours back to Dunedin on Tuesday the 16ᵗʰ, where he has his first and only dose of radiation. They return together that evening.

I hear nothing further from him, but it doesn't stop me sending him photos and short messages. They are of no consequence but are part of the "pretend-all-is-well-and-it-will-be" strategy that I have embraced, like a battered spouse, knowing it's not true.

NOVEMBER 20ᵀᴴ

The French rugby team are playing against the All Blacks from New Zealand. I send recordings of the

All-Blacks Haka and the French Marseillaise. I also record my own excited voice, saying I hope he is up watching the match. He has always loved teasing me about the superiority of the Kiwis over the Frogs, so I worry when he misses the opportunity for some cheap heckling with me.

Silence.

A futile attempt to maintain the pretence that all is well.

It isn't.

NOVEMBER 24TH

I phone my brother-in-law, Craig, who has done the five-plus hour drive from Christchurch and is expecting to drive Ross a further two and a half hours to Dunedin Hospital that day. At last, Ross is to get the first of the "famous" Keytruda infusions that he has been questing so persistently since he heard about the possibility two months back.

But Craig says, in a quiet but grim tone, "I don't think he's going make it, Lynne. It's his call, but it's not looking good." There is a finality to his prediction and I sense the last shot has been fired.

I wish him luck and ask him to keep me posted.

Craig does not drive Ross to Dunedin to get

Keytruda treatment. Instead, my sister drives down to pick up her husband and take him back to Christchurch. She understands very clearly that her brother is not going anywhere. I have lost count of the number of hours driving everyone seems to be doing. I am aware of the amount of organisation that must be going on to keep businesses running, children taken care of, and people fed. Grandparents, friends, and the local community all seem to have morphed into one giant team of "can do" helpers. I wish I were there to do my bit. My sister drives back to Ote on her own on November 27th. She is part of the makeshift home hospital care unit. The only thing she and her niece don't do is administer the morphine.

NOVEMBER 28TH (SUNDAY)

I make my regular Sunday-morning call to Mum in Wanaka. It's a long conversation. I have learned not to push my own feelings for Ross onto my mother. He is her son. He is my brother. I have learned that her story is not my story. I stopped overtly wanting her to embrace him as her long-lost son a long time ago, but in my heart of hearts I know I am still yearning for some kind of closure that will give a "happy ending" to a story that I am a part of but not central to.

"You know Ross didn't go to Dunedin, right?" A delicate approach.

"Yes, I heard from Maxine."

"I heard it's not looking too good." A tiptoe.

"No, it doesn't. Do you think I should go over?" An opening.

"Could be a good idea. Is there anyone who could drive you over the hill? Tomorrow, for example?" An overt nudge.

"Yes, Jean said she would." An immediate response.

I hear she has really given thought to this and wonder why she has not already stated the obvious. Of course, she is going back over the hill to see him. She's already been once, but she wasn't happy with what happened. I don't really understand what she wasn't happy about and now is not then, so I don't care much either. If she is waiting for encouragement from me, I don't give it. The skill of the child is in trying to get the parent to do what she wants without telling her. The skill of the parent is in pretending not to notice the manipulation. That's how it plays out between us now.

"If you do decide to go, try to get a few moments alone with him." A light tone.

I am certain she hears my secret wish for closure and says she will sleep on it. She will "know" in the morning if it is the right thing to do.

NOVEMBER 29ᵀᴴ (MONDAY MORNING)

It is the "right thing to do" and so her friend Jean drives her the ninety minutes over the hill from Wanaka to Otematata. She does spend a few minutes alone with Ross. It's a short visit. I never ask what she says and she never volunteers the information. She does tell me though that she is very pleased that she went; that she recognised in her heart that it was the right thing to do. In my own heart, I pray that there has been closure. I feel intensively relieved—almost happy—as though the breath I have been holding, for what seems like forever, is finally released. I go to bed that Sunday night in France with loosened shoulders and easy breathing.

NOVEMBER 29ᵀᴴ (MONDAY EVENING)

At ten minutes after nine, my brother releases his last breath, his last goal having eluded him: Keytruda treatment.

His wife Petrea, sister Maxine, children James and Emma, and their mother Marilyn surround his bed. There is a large brown frog on the wall high above his head. Frogs, I am told, are rarely seen in the area and never inside a house. This last precious detail described to me later by my sister is something I will latch onto as a kindly wink from God. I was there too.

9H15AM, NOVEMBER 29ᵀᴴ (FRANCE)

I am walking across the square and along a tree-lined path to my office. I have a group online at 9h30. My sister calls me on WhatsApp.

"He's gone," she says.

I could walk to my office blindfolded. It's a three-minute walk from my front door to the lift in the building on the opposite side of the square and up to the eighth floor. I have been doing this walk for the past twelve years. At this time of the year, there are dead leaves everywhere, waiting for the wind to scatter them on or municipal cleaners to sweep them up. My sister's words remove the sensitivity from my feet, the rustle of leaves from my ears and the sight of bare branches from my eyes. Momentarily, I neither see nor hear anything. Automatic pilot guides me to the entrance of my office building. My sister's call is not a conversation; it is simple information. I call my son to give him the information. My words are all mushed up somewhere inside my throat. They come out in gasps and strangled headlines.

"Ross just died," I say. "My brother just died," I add—pointlessly.

There is not much else I can say and nothing much

he can say in return. He lends me kind ears.

My world has changed, but I still take the lift to my office. I still turn on the computer and go into the kitchen, as usual, to make a cup of tea. It is twenty-six minutes past nine. I am not ready to don my smile or drape my sorrow in professional etiquette. I postpone the moment by making another call. I try to tell my best friend that my brother has just died, but the words come out in another mangled mess of gulps and sobs. She listens. There is not much she can say either. I hang up, go to my desk, sit in front of the computer on my ergonomic stool, connect to Zoom, open up the virtual room, and let people in.

23H30, NOVEMBER 29TH (NEW ZEALAND)

The undertakers from Oamaru are on the job. They are in the bedroom with their trolley but they can't get it, with the body on it, out again. It's the stuff of Loony Tunes.

It reminds me of a macabre moment in a cemetery when my friend's body was being buried and the undertakers realised the hole wasn't big enough for the coffin to slip into. I giggle, remembering their struggle to remain dignified whilst making staccato jabs at the hole to marginally enlarge it.

No one at number 57 Rata Drive, Otematata, on the night of November 29th is talking about knocking down a wall, but James does suggest slinging his dad's body over his shoulder in a fireman's hold. He's his father's son: All solutions to problems are just one imaginative thought away. It's easy to imagine Ross chortling, "You can do it, Mate!" Like me, thinking about the undersized hole at the graveyard, everyone is snuffling giggles. It's no longer Ross they are talking about—it's a body, like any other bulky object, that they can't get out the damn door of the ruddy bedroom. I'm not there but I see the Loony Tune scene through others' eyes later.

The house heaves a sigh of relief when it is over. The body is out the door, on a trolley and into the hearse waiting in the driveway. Relief comingles with grief when it gazes at the empty bed. Busy-ness keeps the sense of loss at bay. The absurdity of a house built without ever thinking how the owner would exit it without the help of his living body to manoeuvre the corners is chuckle-worthy.

His body is taken to the morgue in Oamaru. It is well after midnight. Despite my sister's involvement in the drama and her respect for the last moments of our brother's life, she has done her best to include me by phoning me throughout the night with updates.

DECEMBER 3ʳᴰ

My brother lies, still, in his casket at the morgue in Oamaru. I am still in France. New Zealand is still in lockdown.

Maxine calls me on WhatsApp and I join her and Craig at the open casket inside the funeral parlour.

She turns the camera towards the body, lying there dressed in Ross's best suit, floral shirt, and finest tie. It's wearing his metallic blue-rimmed glasses over closed eyes. The suit is too big; the casket, too small for the man I remember. Maxine clucks over it; the eternal mother fussing lovingly around the edges. She pops a wee wooden angel into the box along with a candle and some incense. "To light the way," she says. I murmur a few words of love, of thanks, of farewell to the man who is no longer there. Craig stares, hands in pockets, his grief palpable, even at such a distance.

I remember going to pay my respects to Swami Veetamohananda at the morgue in Paris in 2019. It was a cold, grey, wet, and miserable December day. I hung around outside, under one of Paris's many bridges, waiting to file past his body. I had no more than a few seconds beside his body, which was dressed in the traditional orange robes of a sannyasi.[8] I had spent almost thirty years in his company, but when I looked upon his face, I did not recognise him at all. I don't know which photo the mortician had modelled his work on but the face I was looking at did not resemble in any way the kind, gentle spirit I had loved and respected for so long. It shocked me, at the time.

At least I recognize this face as the one Ross had worn for seventy years and the one I had known for twenty-seven. It looks a little strange to my eyes— maybe it is the stillness. I have never associated stillness with my brother.

---

[8] One who has renounced the world by performing his own funeral and abandoning all claims to social or family standing.

Questions

Have you ever accompanied someone who is dying? What kind of experience was that?

Did you lose anyone during COVID? How did you live that experience?

Have you ever looked upon the face of a departed loved one? How did you feel?

Is it easy, or difficult, for you to think about or discuss dying, death and funerals? What's easy? What's difficult?

How many funerals have you been to? What rituals were the same or different amongst those you have attended?

Think about a loved one. What words would you like to say to that person now, rather than keep them for his or her funeral?

If grief were a garden, what part of the garden would represent grief? How would you, or do you, tend to that part of the garden?

> Are the questions in this section something you are happy to address, or would you rather skip these questions? Can you say why?

PART FOUR

It's No Picnic

JANUARY 19ᵀᴴ, 2023 (NEW ZEALAND)
THE PICNIC TABLE

I'm on my way back to Christchurch from Wanaka and am calling into Otematata to meet Richard Patton, Ross's close friend and MC at his funeral. It's the second time in six months that I have been back to New Zealand. The country opened its borders in April 2022.

Richard meets me in the car park and drives us down to the edge of Lake Benmore, where the mayor and fellow councillors have had a large picnic table built in Ross's memory.

Richard has prepared a picnic and I expect us to wander along the track that leads down to the lake, together, but instead, he turns to me and says, "You go ahead. You might like to spend a little time there on your own."

I appreciate his thoughtfulness. It's been over a year since Ross left us and he mourns his loss as much as I do.

It's a glorious summer day. The sun is high in an early-afternoon sky. Tall poplars line the dirt track, offering a modicum of shade. Richard sits under one of them, close to where he's parked his car. I continue on, on my own, at a languid pace. I don't immediately spot the table, despite its size, because of the way the track drops gently down to the edge of a tiny inlet. A small dinghy tilts to one side on the shore of an adjoining, equally tiny, cove.

The picnic table is big and solid, well screwed down onto a thick concrete base. It's made of pine wood and has a corrugated iron canopy stretched high above the tabletop. Two equally solid wooden benches run along both sides of the table. The whole structure is held in place by steel poles. Eight screws hold a metal plaque at one end of the table. "In Memory of Ross McRobie. Councillor for Ahuriri Ward, Waitaki District Council—2019—2021. Donated by Mayor and Councillors. 'Dedicated to his family and to his community.'" It can seat twelve people comfortably and offer them shade on a hot, sunny day or cover from rain. I take in all the details as if I may never see it again.

I slide gently, reverently, onto one of the benches. I lean forward, spreading my arms wide, palms flat on wood. My hands caress the table's smooth surface. There is no one to hear the few choked howls that get away from me. No one to witness the tears that mess up this idyllic summer scene. No passerby to pick up the words of tenderness and regret that leak into an empty space.

I remember back to his funeral on December 4th, 2021, and the words I spoke then. It had been odd watching myself on video at two o'clock in the morning, sitting up in bed, in France. I gave a good performance sprinkled with light humour and no tears. I had begun by saying that he did numbers; our sister, pictures; and me, words. I then quoted some numbers: two mothers, two sisters, two children, three wives. I was teasing him even then.

Mine had been the last of the speeches before the slides, showing my brother at various stages of his life. I imagined it was not an uncommon occurrence for family members to see their children or siblings through the eyes of others for the first time. In my case, I saw the first forty years of my brother's life on screen and found out what his favourite music was. I knew he played the piano but didn't know that he was an accomplished pianist who had competed with the best.

Sitting at his empty picnic table beside the lake, I can still hear the bold, clear voice of his beautiful seven-year-old granddaughter, Olivia, speaking to the packed hall.

"I appreciate you all coming here today for the death of my granddad. My granddad was the best, like when he slipped in the pool or when he forgot to put the bung in the boat and it started to fill up with water. We all know he will be the brightest star in the sky and shine down on us. Now let's give a clap for my granddad to tell him how much we appreciate him."

Everybody did.

Her love and the peacefulness of the little inlet pull me back from the brink of melancholy. The clear lake water ripples indolently on a pebbled shoreline. The surrounding hills and lakeside grasses repeat themselves like slightly ruffled mirrors under a dazzlingly blue sky. The only sound I pick up is the lazy buzz-hum of a hot summer afternoon.

Richard quietly joins me at the table and brings out our lunch. He's thought of everything, including a vegetarian option. We don't really know each other at all but he is deeply respectful of what this moment means to me. We share anecdotes about Ross. We both have a chuckle over the appropriate size of the table for a man like Ross, who never did things in half measures. We both can see him, presiding over the table, standing up to make a welcome speech to all picnic attendees, totally in his element at the head of the table or standing at the lake edge, sun behind him, arms out, voice booming.

"I bet he was pissed off he didn't get to make the opening speech at his own funeral," I quip. We both laugh, recognising the element of truth in that statement.

We start swapping stories about the funeral.

"Was it you who told the yarn about Ross and the notorious Shaw triplets in a car chase?"

"Yeah, Keith couldn't make the funeral, so I read it out for him."

"The Bro' really was a confident devil, wasn't he? Or he was just an inveterate show-off who resisted a challenge as well as a bull did a red flag?"

"Bit of both, I think, Lynne." Richard laughs, remembering the yarn.

Ross and his mate Keith were still in high school and had "lucked out" at a Saturday night dance in Invercargill. They were on their way home in Ross's sports car when a Mark 3 Zephyr came alongside them at a traffic light.

No way he would have had a sports car if he'd grown up in our family, I remember thinking as I followed the story about what happened after Ross had given the fingers to three lads in the Zephyr.

How bloody stupid was that? The entire funeral gathering was tittering, asking themselves the same question. *Red flag to a bull,* was the unspoken consensus.

I gave a loud guffaw when Richard, the storyteller, revealed that my testosterone-driven brother had not only just given three lads the fingers but had chosen to give them to the city's biggest thug trio. "Hello!"

Richard and I are still laughing about the ending of the story as we munch our way through our picnic.

"Who but my brother would get involved in a car chase with a notorious gang? And I bet he loved the adrenaline rush, revving the engine and careening around corners at breakneck speed."

"They were both scared shitless and thought they'd end as pulp on the road when the gang finally cornered them," Richard reminds me.

"How did it end again?"

"All five lads got out of their cars. Ross and Keith were expecting their comeuppance. The head honcho swaggered up to them and asked who the driver was."

"Oh yeah, I remember holding my breath with the rest of the crowd. I loved the way you played the suspense, Richard." We both chuckle, remembering that moment in the story.

"The guy says, 'That was the best car chase we've ever had. We're lettin' y' go!' and he turns and saunters back to the Zephyr."

"He was a lucky devil as well being a confident one, then," I conclude, answering my earlier question.

This is precious time I am sharing with Richard. We're remembering the great guy we have both lost. Laughing about his impossibly larger-than-life character and all his foibles brings him alive to us, sitting at his memorial picnic table. Laughing is a panacea for grief.

There is still a long car drive back to Christchurch ahead of me, so by unspoken agreement, Richard packs up the leftovers and we wander back along the path to the car park. Ripe wild wheat grasses stand tall on the bank of Lake Avimore's boat harbour. Feathery fronds of giant toitoi waver idly in an almost imperceptible afternoon breeze. It is an ideal place for people to come in memory of my brother or just to sit and enjoy a picnic with friends. One day, someone reading the plaque will ask who he was and there will be no one left to explain.

"He was either a big shot or loved enough for someone to want to erect this whopping great picnic table in his memory," they may say.

I will not be there to tell them that he was both to me—that my dedication would have been "Met so late. Left too soon."

Richard drives us back to the township. He walks me round the streets to Ross's house, to his own place and to the community centre hall where Ross's funeral was held. I see it full of the mourners I watched on my computer screen in the middle of a cold winter night in 2021.

I see my ninety-one-year-old mother walk in rapidly, head bowed. She is flanked by my sister and her husband. She is dressed in a long floral summer dress with matching short beige jacket. I see only her stooped back. She sits, cocooned, between Maxine and Craig at the end of the front row. She had climbed Mount Iron on her ninetieth birthday and drank champagne at the top with her grandson, Christophe. I remember wondering as I watched her walk in, how she would deal with this. While I trusted her pride to keep her upright, I wondered if this was yet another injustice that would join the graveyard of unaddressed pain thrust deep beneath her bones.

I snap out of it and say to Richard, in a jocular tone, "He was a stubborn bastard, wasn't he?"

Richard looks a bit taken back, wondering where that comment suddenly popped up from.

"Well, he was certainly a very determined chap." He looks at me quizzically, waiting for me to say more.

We're still standing outside the community hall and what has popped up are the stories people told about how, once Ross had made up his mind to do something, he wouldn't let anything get in his way. They didn't say it quite like that. They heralded his mantra "Set the Goal, Get the Goal." His son, James, had lauded the way his dad had "smashed out his real estate study in record time." His daughter, Emma, shared a couple of funny anecdotes about her dad and his obstinacy. One was about a fight they'd had in Italy. He had been determined to get a photo of her holding up the Tower of Pisa and she, equally stubborn, "wasn't having a bar of it." The other story was about his introduction to her future husband at the local driving range. Ross, undaunted by his ignorance of golf, wanted to teach her "how to do it." His insistence met with a whack on the head when she teed off, dutifully following his instructions. His future son-in-law was welcomed into the family amidst blood and expletives. Neither injury nor foul language stopped the pair of them becoming good mates. Ross could be "dripping blood" or about to be thrashed, yet still he could compel others to like him by the sheer force of his smile and his "nothing-is-ever-as-bad-as-you-think" attitude.

Both Emma and James commented on their father's addiction to speed. James, by teasing him about having a midlife crisis when he bought an MGBGT; Emma, by acknowledging what was deeply painful for everyone — the speed of his departure from life. James acknowledged his dad's love of car racing and had recognised how good he was on the bends when Ross had taken him on a few laps of the local car-racing circuit.

"You didn't muck around, Dad." Emma had spoken tenderly, looking to his coffin. "And in the end, it worked in your favour. The last four days were extremely difficult but we did our best and I know you were grateful, Dad."

The yarn about the car race made sense. The speed with which he left us made sense too. He never mucked around and he never had difficulty expressing gratitude.

"Funerals are wonderful, aren't they?" I muse out loud. Richard, who hasn't been following my inner dialogue, again, looks a bit mystified but goes along with my train of thought anyway.

"This one was exceptional," he says, "given the short amount of time in which the service was put together. It was a colossal task for his kids and Petrea. They were dealing with COVID restrictions and a guest list a mile long."

"True, but I was thinking more about the way funerals allow us to eulogize a person's life. I hope Ross heard all those great things people said about him, lying there in his casket."

"I think he would have been wondering when the hell we were going to pour the wine, Lynne." Richard gave a chuckle.

"He would have been pissed off not to get the last word," I joke. We both smile, thinking about the guy who loved to share a glass or two and gave as good as he got.

"I miss our evening chats down at the lake on the boat," Richard says, a little wistfully. "We shared many deep and personal thoughts over a few glasses of wine.

He really was a good mate to me."

I feel Richard's nostalgia. It matches mine but, in reality, I never had those long meaningful conversations with Ross. I got close to having one when we spent two days cycling together between Lake Pukaki and Otematata back in January 2017. I guess I had always thought there would time for those kinds of chats.

I'm remembering the way each speaker adorned my dead brother with memories wrought in gold and precious stones. He did indeed shine in their words like the star in a night sky, alluded to in his golden-haired granddaughter's speech.

Death is a dark space that we fill with love and light. A funeral, a time for collective amnesia and euphoria. Ross's funeral was just that. His friends remembered his madcap adventures, his generosity, his determination, the way he really did want the very best for everyone he came across. His family turned his misadventures into humorous anecdotes. Their stories were winks to love, not digs of disappointment. They loved him, warts and all.

I knew him to be a powerful magnet who easily drew people into his orbit. It was almost a given that he would eventually be drawn into local politics. People basked in his aura but, at times, his recklessness and insatiable appetites led the unwary to precipitous edges that were not always easy to pull back from. They were dark places, where those who loved him stopped laughing and had to search within themselves for a place of forgiveness. Those memories did not belong at his funeral. They were enclosed in his coffin and burned with his body. Wind, water, and earth swallowed them along with his ashes.

The picnic table is where those who knew him, for better or for worse, would go in memory of him. My thoughts sway lazily, like wet seaweed in a rock pool; sometimes slimy, mostly graceful, in the afternoon sun, chatting to Richard.

He changes the subject. "I'm enjoying reading your book. Some of the questions you ask have really got me thinking."

Asking questions is what my job as a coach is about, but I'm pleased to hear that they "work" for a reader. I peppered my first book with them. They were invitations to come with me on a pilgrimage, not only to the tomb of Saint James in Santiago, but also to the heart of one's self. I had walked there over the course of four years, three seasons, and ten days with another Richard, a long time ago.[9]

"I'm really glad you like it." I'm grinning like the proverbial Cheshire cat. "You know," I add, "Ross

---

[9] Described in detail in my first book, *Once a Pilgrim, Always a Coach*.

would probably never have read my book, even if he had lived to see it published, but I'm damned sure he would have told 'the world' about his 'sister from Paris who writes books.'"

"Yes, he was pretty proud of having a sister living in Paris," Richard agrees.

"I'll never know now if 'writing books' would have scored over 'living in Paris' but I do know there would have been nothing wry about his enthusiasm. He just had an amazing capacity to fire up belief in someone about something."

"Yep, that was Ross." Richard grins too. "That's why we all loved him and why we won't forget him."

The two of us say goodbye and agree to meet up again the next time I am back this way.

THE DRIVE—MULL TIME

It's a fast trip back up State Highway 83 to the junction in Omarama where the road joins up with the main route north. It's only a twenty-four-kilometre detour from the north-south artery of the South Island. I top up the tank of my frog-green Toyota rental in Omarama. I didn't choose the colour. It had been near impossible to rent anything on four wheels in New Zealand in 2022. Rental car companies had divested of much of their fleets in a pandemic world and couldn't meet demand in a world on the move again. I had been lucky to find "Kermit." He had been built for small Japanese ladies and not for their long-legged Kiwi sisters. When I pull out of the gas station and head off north towards the inland lakes, I know I will be making frequent stops to stretch my legs.

I mull over the past eighteen months as I drive alone. I think about what Richard had said about my book and what my mother's reaction had been to it.

She had never finished reading my book. She had enjoyed telling people her daughter was writing a book about walking the Way of Saint James. But when she actually began to read the unpublished manuscript, she realised that it wasn't only a travelogue. She told me she didn't like it. I remember feeling surprised and hurt. When I questioned her further, she said it depressed her. At the time of the conversation, the manuscript was still with the proofreader. I still had time to scrabble through the first few scenes, looking for anything she might have found offensive. I found an anecdote about walking home, alone, in the dark, on a winter's night. I was writing about how my friend Jesus walked with me so I wouldn't be afraid. I was musing about what other people used as a talisman to manage their fears when they were growing up. I had referred to childhood in general, and mine in particular, as an "urban warehouse." I realised, on re-reading it, that I loved the sound of the words, but the statement itself wasn't true. It was easy to cross them out. The image never made it to print.

We were on another Sunday-morning call when I asked her again what it was that she didn't like about my story. She hedged but finally said that she had always thought my childhood had been happy.

"But it was," I insisted, over the phone. "What makes you think it wasn't?"

"I must have been a terrible mother." She avoided the question.

"What, in the book, makes you say that?" I felt guilty of something that wasn't being named.

"I don't know," she began. "... letting you come home alone in the dark," she finished a bit lamely.

I felt sad that I could never take away her sense of failure as a mother, despite my succeeding in almost everything I ever put my mind to. She had always been proud of my successes as if they were her own. My story, my book, was about me, and not her.

But she was experiencing it as her failure, and not my success. I understood that she was possibly afraid of what else she might discover if she kept reading the story. She was still, and by choice, the publicly unacknowledged mother of Ross. She remained isolated in the pain and shame of an event that went back more than seventy years. It wasn't something that my existence could heal, despite years of unconscious effort. No, my childhood was definitely not unhappy; it had just been missing a piece.

"It's my story, Mum, not yours," I told her as gently as I could.

DOWN AT THE LAKE (EVENING, JANUARY 19ᵀᴴ)

My eyes haven't left the landscape or the road, even if my mind momentarily has gone elsewhere for a few kilometres. This drive is spectacular. Nature is at her stunning best. I pull into the car park overlooking Lake Pukaki. It's already gone five o'clock in the afternoon. All the tourist buses have left and the picnic benches are empty. A few people are clambering over rocks at the edge of the water. Golden wheat grasses shimmer close to the lake's turquoise waters. Mount Aoraki, dressed in perennial white, stares down the lake with regal aplomb. The mount cuts a clean figure against a blank blue sky. Its nakedness exacts reverence from those lucky enough to see it without its usual cloud throwover. I take the time to stop and look, not caring much about the three-hour drive still ahead.

BIRTHDAYS

The last time I came through here was with my sister on my seventieth birthday, in July, in the middle of winter, only six months ago. I had spent the whole of 2022 celebrating my birthday in some form or another. That year had felt like any excuse would do, to celebrate being alive in a post-pandemic and brotherless world.

I was born in the freezing cold of a New Zealand winter, three weeks into July. I hate cold birthdays. I only remember one of the twenty-two New Zealand birthdays I had.

On my fifth birthday, my mother threw a kids' party for me. There were balloons and cakes and little sausages on sticks. What I remember most were the small triangles of thin, white bread covered in thousands of tiny multi-coloured sugar balls. I licked them off the bread and, before they melted, I ran around the house, tongue out, roaring and clawing. All the other kids thought this was a great game and joined in. My sugar-soaked buddies and I were having the time of our lives, stoking pandemonium. It could have been our sticky fingers on the wallpaper or just the sheer volume of the noise that brought the party to an end. I don't remember.

And I don't remember any other parties. Our family house was naturally silent. It didn't like having its insides disturbed. It rejected noisy children or anything that could spoil its tidy surface. Coal fires, kerosene heaters, hot water bottles between cotton sheets were all part of bleak Christchurch winters. Parties were not. In the summer, playing outside didn't disturb anyone, but that wasn't when my birthday was.

I had to come to Europe to enjoy my birthdays. I love summer birthdays. That must be the reason why I never went back to live in New Zealand. I had only two other winter birthdays: my forty-second when I met my brother and my seventieth when I came home to say goodbye to my mother.

Questions

What kind of ceremony would you like to have to mark the passage of your life on Earth?

When you leave the body you have spent your life in, would you like it to be buried or cremated? If cremated, where would you like your ashes to lie?

How would you like your life to be remembered?

If you were to write an ethical will now, what kind of moral or spiritual heritage would you like to leave for those who come after you?

Could you write that ethical will now?

What story of your life do you most want to tell? Could you write it down? What's stopping you?

What kind of memorial would be a fitting tribute to your life?

Who is your most cherished friend? What makes him or her that most cherished friend?

PART FIVE

It's a Long Way Home

THE NEWS, APRIL 2022

I pick up the phone for our usual Sunday-morning chat. She says she has been to see her doctor, who has given her the results of some tests she had done. Her friend Jean is with her for our call this morning. It is an awkward conversation.

"They weren't too good."

I recognize the euphemism and let go of a small but imperceptible sigh.

"So, what did your doctor tell you?" I push for facts to quell a rising sense of foreboding.

"It's in the vulva and spreading fast." She too, prefers facts to feelings. "There's no cure."

How many more? I feel close to despair, wondering how many more people I love are going to get on the train and leave me standing on the platform, alone.

I don't know how to ask the obvious question. It feels too brutal. So, instead of saying, "How long have you got?" I ask, "What's Christmas looking like at this stage?"

She understands perfectly what I am really asking and says she'll put me on to Jean, who was also with her at the doctor's surgery. "I'm still a wee bit upset."

She hands the phone over to her friend, who gives me a verbatim rundown of the conversation with the doctor. The medical terms flummox me and I'm not sure I want to know anyway.

"Jean, I have a ticket to New Zealand for Christmas but should I change it and come earlier?"

It's easier to be upfront with a friend than with my mother. I want to be practical and grown-up but the little child that I still am inside does not want her mother to leave her. I see me, a child on a beach, scooping frantically with my bare hands to empty a sand hole of seawater. The more I scoop, the more the water rushes in. My heart feels like a sand hole with grief rushing in from all sides. I want to keep it out.

Jean says, in a matter-of-fact tone, "Errrmm, Lynne, I think you had better come before. Christmas is a long way off." The Irish lilt of her voice softens what I feel to be true. There isn't much time left. But how much time?

"What if I were to come in July?" I ask tentatively, my mind doing some wild calculations about how I could make that work with the grandchildren, my job, the months of planning my husband has put into taking me to the Scottish Highlands for a special birthday treat in August.

"I wouldn't leave it any later than that."

I see Death as feminine, as part of the earth cycle: creating, nourishing, decaying, and dying. Once her bell begins to toll, she will set her own pace, ignoring my work-life schedule. She is not open to negotiation. Even if I were to ignore her, as we all chose to do for the last three months of my brother's life, she would still follow her own timetable. She has the last word.

The tragedy of the moment is lightened by both Jean and Mum joking about going round town sporting T-shirts that read, "Be Kind to Me—I'm Dying." They feel they have finally found the ultimate retort for rude shop assistants, disinterested car park attendants, and slack waiters. I join in the hilarity, adding my tuppence worth. "Yeah, don't forget to wear it when you want a table in a full coffee shop!" I enjoy the relief of laughter that assuages a sagging heart.

That was April.

I put off dealing with it for a month and then at the end of May, I took a hard decision. I cancelled my holiday at the beach with my granddaughters. I didn't exchange my Christmas ticket to New Zealand. I kept it and bought another one for mid-July when my last professional engagement ended. And I said "yes" to my husband's birthday gift of a trip to the land of my ancestors.

HOME AGAIN, JULY 2022

So, there I was on July 18th, 2022, at Charles de Gaulle Airport amidst the chaos of determined-to-travel-again Europeans and a hopelessly understaffed workforce. I ignored all pretence at queuing and feigned urgent business at the check-in counter. A business-class ticket was persuasive for a harassed and outsourced airline staff. My benign smile peppered with smatterings of French and English saved me from being lynched by other customers.

I had only ventured once into the world of foreign travel since the first lockdown in 2020. I flew from Paris-Orly to Jordan at the end of March 2022. I had always wanted to see Petra. It was on my bucket list. So, when friends said they were going for three weeks and I was free of work the week they would be in Petra and the desert, I leapt at the opportunity to join them. It felt providential after two years of lockdowns. I had my vaccination passes to show and my temperature was taken as I entered the airport. I was wearing the obligatory face mask but wondered to what purpose when I saw the deserted halls of the airport. It had been a spooky experience.

It was different by the time July came around and the entire world seemed to be pushing its way to an airline counter to escape, to anywhere other than where one was.

I was happy where I was, in France, in summer. I would have liked to escape, going to New Zealand in the middle of winter but knew this was "it." And I knew that I needed to go.

While I had accepted, like an obedient sheep, that I could not get into the country to see my brother before he died, the outrage that had accumulated got projected onto the New Zealand Travel Pass. I felt irrationally angry that I, a bona fide New Zealand citizen, returning to her own country, had to produce such a certificate or risk being refused entry. It was senseless to waste energy on the issue, but like many others who were accustomed to democratic freedom, I objected to feeling controlled.

I touched down July 20th and headed south with my sister the next day. On July 20th it hadn't been certain that we would be able to get through to Wanaka. Winter weather conditions often meant that roads were flooded, bridges washed away, and mountain passes closed. But that particular day an erstwhile inhospitable landscape was transformed beneath the sun's winter rays. She glared white on rock, blue on high, and gleam on the long straight road through the snow-spotted tussock land of the McKenzie Basin. It was a day made in heaven. We pulled into the car park at Lake Tekapo and "banged into" Ross's daughter, Emma, and her family. They were heading north. We'd arrived at the halfway point at the same time.

"Small world, huh?" We greeted each other, congratulating ourselves on our good fortune. And if that wasn't enough proof of an eminently benevolent universe, Ross's widow Petrea pulled into the same car park a few minutes later. She, too, was heading north but not as far as Emma and her family.

"Needed to give the dog a run," she explained. "Great timing, eh?" Coincidences like these remind me that the Big One running the show definitely has a kind heart.

Petrea was trying to sell their house in Otematata and was towing a trailer load of stuff back up to Christchurch. Petrea shows me "our wiseman" who is also making his way up to Christchurch in the back of the trailer. He is destined for a place next to the TV in Maxine and Craig's house. He will hold the story of our brother delicately between his fingertips with the same care as he holds his lotus.

She needed to start her life again, after a year threaded with grief and turmoil. I didn't envy her.

I thought I'd experienced something akin to her sense of loss prior to my leaving NZ for the first time back in 1975. The man I had loved enough to want him as my life partner had gone to Germany to pursue a fabulous job opportunity. I was devastated when he left. Nothing could fill the empty hole that had opened up in my life; it just grew bigger with each passing month. It was well before electronic messaging could create a semblance of proximity, so time passed without news or fondness. But I was young and resilient. I bounced back after a year of mourning and prepared my own departure. I never returned to live in NZ. The decision may not have been solely motivated by a desire to celebrate birthdays in the sun.

I thought of Petrea as resilient. I was sure she would find a way through her loss and pain. We took a lot of pictures of us all, smiling like the sun, with a brilliant backdrop of mountain and lake.

My sister and I made it easily over the Lindis Pass and down into Wanaka just after dark.

WANAKA IN WINTER

When she knew for sure I was coming, Mum told me that she wanted to make me a special birthday dinner to celebrate my seventieth. This meant "choose your favourite."

"Fish 'n' chips from that place down on the waterfront." Zero hesitation.

By the time Maxine and I drove into the township, it was dark and the streets were deserted. We went straight to the fish 'n' chip shop, picked them up while they were still hot inside their wrapping and headed up the hill to where Mum lived at cottage number four.

"We have to eat them out of the packet, or it doesn't count," I declared on arrival.

"Yes, but they are not wrapped in newspaper either," my sister pointed out. "We could actually serve them on a plate and eat them with a knife and fork."

"Whaaaat? You can't eat fish 'n' chips with a knife and fork. Sacrilege!" I feigned mock horror. "Look, I'm willing to accept that we're no longer back in the good ol' days when fish 'n' chips were handed over the counter wrapped in yesterday's newspaper. But there is no way I'm going to eat them with a knife and fork." Then, I proclaimed the historical law of fish 'n' chip eating: "They have to be eaten with our fingers.

"Anyway, it's my birthday, so I decide."

"And how old did you decide you were today?" my sister demanded, imperiously, and with a big grin.

"Oh, let the kid have her way." Mum helped herself to a chip with her fingers. "I'm cutting the fish with a knife, mind you," she added with a wink.

It was good to be home. It was good to be together. It was good to eat fish 'n' chips in my fingers straight from the packet.

Mum had bought a gigantic cake, which she had iced herself with the words "Happy Birthday Lynne."

"Not allowed to cry on your birthday." Both Mum and Maxine chanted the familiar mantra when they saw my eyes well up. I noticed how thin my mother had become since I'd last seen her in March 2020, just before the world shut down. She hadn't been a very big person, even then. The cancer was sucking the flesh off her bones, and I was a seventy-year-old kid eating my mum's birthday cake, not allowed to cry on my birthday.

OUT AND ABOUT

After my indefinite departure at the end of 1975, I had never gone back to New Zealand without a holiday plan in mind. There was always something to do, somewhere to go, someone to see. This time I had come back with the sole purpose of spending time with my mother. My only wish was to do exactly what she wanted to do, go wherever she wanted to go, be with whomever she wanted to be with. She didn't believe me, at first, and kept coming up with ideas that she thought would please me.

One day, I drove her and her friend Jean all the way up the Lakes Wanaka and Hawea and on to Makarora on the promise of shouting them a coffee when we got there. It was only an hour's drive to Makarora, but it was such a glorious day that we had to make frequent stops for pictures. The stops added forty more minutes to the drive, so by the time we reached our destination, anticipation for a cup of coffee was high. There wasn't a soul in sight. The coffee shop and the gas station were both closed. There was nothing to do, except turn around and drive back home again. We stopped for lunch at a pub in Hawea, but like a lot of tourist venues all over the country post-COVID, staff was in short supply. The food was under par; Mum hardly touched her meal. Not that I blamed her. It had probably been cooked by someone's cousin who had taken the day off from his regular office job to help out. The view up the lake was spectacular so, despite the food, it was worth the stop.

I thought we'd had a wonderful day, but when Mum and I were sitting together, having a cuppa at the end of the afternoon, she told me how ill she had felt all day. She was still getting used to the impact of morphine on a system unused to anything other than the occasional aspirin. That was when I realised that she had said "yes" to the road trip thinking she was pleasing me. She was. I had really enjoyed the trip but I had also imagined I was doing it for her. I hadn't seen any sign of her malaise. In fact, I had no memory of my mother ever being ill. I held her in my mind's eye as a paragon of health. I updated my inner landscape and decided on much shorter trips for subsequent outings.

A few days later, I drove her twenty-five kilometres up the main road to the Cardona Pub for lunch on another beautiful day. She loved the place. It was one of New Zealand's oldest, and she had brought many friends to the pub over the years. She had moved to Wanaka a decade earlier in a state of post-traumatic shock after earthquakes had wrecked the city of Christchurch.

When we got there, it was full of skiers, clattering around on wooden floorboards, chattering nineteen to the dozen. Mum looked overwhelmed by the noise and very small amidst the bulky ski clobber and clunky snow boots.

"I don't like our chances, do you? Maybe we should go somewhere else," she said. It was unlike her to give up before even trying. She was usually the one to knock aside obstacles. Mum expressing negativity, even in small doses, was new territory to me.

"I'll find something," I reassured her while thinking, *I'll play the "My-mother-is-dying" card if I have to.* I scouted around and managed to bag a table near a window. We squeezed into the corner table and waited for our soup to be delivered. The soup was good, but Mum's appetite was, by then, like that of a sparrow. I caught a glimpse of her face when she didn't know I was looking. It had no mask, no public display of cheerfulness. Her gaze was turned towards the window and was one of wistfulness. Who knows what she was thinking; I did not offer a penny for her thoughts. I just remember I felt so very sad amidst the bustle and rustle of ski dungarees and ruddy faces.

Most days during that last July and August we met with her friends downtown for a coffee. She was a specialist at ordering café lattes, which she never fully drank because they got cold. She would ask for a small jug of boiling water to be brought to the table but would then refuse to drink the rest of the latte because she no longer liked it. At least she was consistent in her ability to annoy me with inconsequential details like wasting her coffee. My sister got mad with her refusal to follow her doctor's pain management prescriptions. But her dilemma was clear: She was afraid to lose clarity of thought under the influence of morphine and therefore independence of action. She insisted that she would get by with the pain for as long as possible.

When someone scores their pain level on a scale of 1 to 10, what does that really mean? Mum scored herself above 7 but refused the prescribed amount of morphine. She took a token sip morning and night, as if to please her doctor (or her daughter). It was as if she were saying, "See me being a good girl." None of us bought the ruse.

I chose to trust her willpower over and above the little bottle sitting on the kitchen counter. She was a stubborn and courageous woman, but she didn't make it easy for those who wanted to be in charge of her welfare.

At around the same time she and her friend had been laughing about having the "Be Kind" T-shirts made, she had stated, somewhat grandly, that there be "no funeral when I'm gone." Now that both my sister and I were there, we confronted her with her desire to have a party rather than a funeral.

"True or not true?" Kids (regardless of age) can be merciless with their parents. I pushed her for a decision that she didn't want to make but which we could not make for her.

"Why do you want a party now rather than a funeral later? Apart from the obvious: here for the party and gone for the funeral." Say it like it is. You have to have a leather hide to survive some conversations with your kids.

"I don't know. It's different. No one else I know has done this." Her expression was one of doubt—and of excitement.

I didn't know if she was showing me the persona she had developed during her time in Wanaka or if I was finally seeing the "real" her. She was a groundbreaker, a model for other people, a positive force for life and health. Of course she wanted a Celebration of Life party before her life ended.

She didn't want weeping—she wanted whoopee!

It was one thing to say it but another thing to do it. My sister was plugging for something small at home; something we could cater ourselves without too much fuss. She was in favour of low key and low cost.

"Look, they're all over seventy." She sounded reasonable. "They won't want to drink champagne in the middle of the afternoon. Tea and coffee will be fine."

"How many people do you think are likely to come?" I was looking at the size of the lounge in her cottage and wondering if we could stagger arrivals if Mum invited more than ten people. "We haven't got enough chairs," I pointed out. My reasonable tone of voice matched my sister's. "They will need to sit down at that age." I had totally forgotten that I too had just turned seventy.

"It's only going to be for a couple of hours and people won't stay that long anyway. It's dark by five o'clock." Maxine sounded sure of herself, but it didn't fit with my idea of "whoopee."

The what and the where would determine the who. I didn't like faffing around, and time was short. I was leaving Wanaka on August 12th. The decision had to be Mum's, but it was as if she couldn't give herself permission to say what she really wanted in front of her two daughters (who had different ideas on the subject). It was as if she had to favour one daughter over the other and she didn't want to do that. Kids can be unforgiving judges of their parents, so she could be forgiven for being hesitant in expressing her wishes. Instead of deciding the what and the where, she focused on the who. But that depended on the what and the where—and around we went again. She didn't want to forget anyone but couldn't invite everyone she knew in town. She didn't know where to draw the line. And she was trying to make decisions while her body was suffering from intense pain, which she refused to treat with stronger doses of morphine. However, the longer her guest list grew, the less likely a "home do" got.

Until finally ... "I was thinking of something a wee bit fancy, down by the lake." Mum ventured forth with her idea as though she had just thought of it. "Something in a nice lounge at Edgewater, overlooking the lake," she continued, clearly indicating that she had thought about it and knew exactly what she wanted. "Petits fours, champagne, music. Tea and coffee, of course.

Sparkling water too." And as if to justify her extravagant wishes, she added, "I will use the money I have put aside for a funeral to pay for it."

There wasn't a lot we could say after that. That was a decision.

"I'll call Edgewater and ask for a quote." It was to be for an afternoon party on August 11th for fifty people; champagne, tea and coffee; sweet and savoury finger foods; a room overlooking the lake.

"How much, please?"

PARTY PREPARATION

Procrastination over, the worrying began. This hotel was also suffering from staff shortages. It was winter and their employees were on leave. I had three different email contacts and never the same person twice over the phone. Fed up with organisers' anxiety, the three of us just showed up at the hotel reception desk one day and requested personalised attention. All our worries melted with the appearance of a manager who fell over backwards to be of service. He told us he was about to return to India to celebrate his grandmother's birthday.

"But not to worry. Your party will go perfectly well in my absence. I will make sure of it," he reassured us with his big smile and Indian accent.

"My grandmother's dying, you see, so I have to go," he said in way of explanation for his absence. We didn't like to spell out in capitals that Mum, like his grandmother, wasn't long for this world either. I'm not sure he quite got that the party he was organising for the woman in the spunky gear fit for a forty-year-old, sitting opposite him, was in lieu of a funeral for that same woman. He wanted to do a good job and he, personally, would make sure Mum got the party she wanted. We chatted numbers. We simulated room layout. We visualised the flow of guests and staff. We talked timings and worst-case scenarios. We imagined solutions. We spent time. I couldn't imagine this amount of undivided attention being afforded us in a mega-metropolis like Paris.

We left the hotel feeling confident and cheerful. In my book, he ranked as the world's number one manager: friendly, helpful, thorough. I experienced his service as genuine and not just professional. Admittedly, Mum had turned her charm thermostat up to high and, just possibly, semi-consciously, he had been spoiling his own grandmother back in India.

The venue sorted, we were then free to worry about the speeches and the playlist. I began to see the advantage of a funeral when it came to writing a eulogy for my mother. I was sure that Ross would have approved of all the wonderful things said about him at his funeral (not that he could have done anything about it!). Mum, on the other hand, wanted full control of what was to be said. I was proud of the chequered working career Mum had had. She, to me, was someone who could turn her hand to any job that was offered. She had held secretarial positions, managerial positions, and a multitude of sales jobs—including cars, Building Society shares, makeup, bedding, et al. But she absolutely did not want any of that to be mentioned.

"It's nobody's business what I have done with my life." She was irked and on the defensive.

Her irritation made me wonder to what extent she had wrapped up her former lives in a sheath of "mystique." To what degree had she "re-invented" herself since leaving Christchurch after Dad's death ten years earlier? What could I genuinely say about her? I appreciated discretion but couldn't abide by secrets; I knew firsthand that knowledge withheld from family members was damaging. Given my profession, I'd had a lot more practice at self-revelation than my mother, and wanted her permission to do some revealing. I really wanted to tell her story, but who was I to lay down the law to my mother?

"Do you want me to say anything or not?" I hadn't managed to swallow my annoyance. I had shrunk to the four-foot kid I once was, hand on hips, glaring. I resented being told what I could and could not say.

"Yes, of course I do." She sounded sulky.

"So, dictate to me what you want me to say," I said in a perfunctory tone. I still wasn't standing very tall.

"Oh, say what you want!" The tone was snooty sharp.

The terse exchange, bordering on bitchiness, was followed by a sullen silence. I hated her.

After a few minutes, I grew up again.

"Mum, you have had such a rich life and a multitude of jobs—don't you want people to know that? I'm really proud of all that you have done with your life." I found a placatory voice. She wouldn't budge.

"Yes, but I've not been to university or anything like that," she argued. She didn't feel good enough in whose company? I wasn't about to go there.

"So, out of all those jobs you've done, which are the ones that stand out for you? Which ones do you feel most proud of yourself?" I heard the manipulative coach guiding the conversation towards a desired outcome. My desired outcome! Kids cannot be coaches to their parents.

"Well, I was the first non-nursing woman to be named by the matron-in-chief as the nurses' supervisor at the public hospital."

I didn't know that! Parents, I knew, took great interest in their kids' lives but how much interest did their kids take in them? How old did one have to be to realize that their stories would leave with them? How many other things had my mother not told me about herself just because I never thought to ask? Time felt so short.

"That's great, Mum, so I'll just say one or two things that you'd like me to say and I'll keep it short and simple. That OK?" I understood she was struggling to keep a hold on a life that was escaping her. Exerting a little control over what I said about her, to her friends, was a small way of still feeling she was the elder and could impose her terms.

The smart phone was mine. The loudspeaker was mine. I controlled the playlist. I was magnanimous with inclusion rights. Mum got The Andrew Sisters; Maxine got Simple Minds; Craig, Men Without Hats; and I got the rest. I swiftly consulted on my choices and found everyone, miraculously, to be in agreement.

"Don't you think The Andrew Sisters are bit too old for everyone?" Mum suddenly doubted her choice. I didn't remind her that most of her guests would be over seventy or eighty and that her age would surpass them all by at least ten years.

One morning not long before the party, we tuned into the local radio station. They were playing the '60s hit, "It's My Party." Mum and I let loose on the refrain, bellowing out, "You would cry too if it happened to you!" followed by hoots of laughter. That one got downloaded. The party made sense. It was a celebration of life and laughter; of joy and song; of the lightness of being. Even if Mum was having second thoughts about inviting people to a party rather than asking them to attend her funeral, I held her to her initial idea of doing something different. She was an over-ninety trailblazer and I was proud of her.

The invitations went out from my French email address, which meant some went into spam boxes and never got read. Others were sent back with "unable to deliver" headings, which meant revising the list of guests. A simple task turned into a lengthy process. Phone calls had to replace email efficiency. This meant conversations and explanations. It wasn't easy to call and say, "Oh, by the way, I'm dying and I'd love you to come to my party to celebrate that." So, the conversations were elaborate chats around "I'm throwing an afternoon party down at the lake and I'm inviting a few friends. I'd love you to come."

Amidst the flurry of party organising, there were visits from the palliative care team, the cancer team, and other caregivers. They left pamphlets that explained the dying process: what to expect and when. The words were clear and the pictures helpful. Meanwhile, Mum was continuing to score her pain in the over-7 range while tinkering nominally with liquid morphine, morning and night.

"I'd rather talk about the party," she said after one of these visits when she had felt badgered about her lack of assiduity over her morphine doses. The party helped her focus on the positive in much the same way Ross had focused on selling houses or joining a board.

"Let's talk about the party," I willingly agreed. A party was something to look forward to, something that took our minds off all the "other stuff." It was easier for me to treat the party as a professional event that I had been asked to facilitate because that put me on familiar turf: a deadline, a focus, and clear objectives. My job was to keep the champagne flowing, the music going, the speeches short and to trust the process. I could rely on Mum to play her role as "hostess with the mostest." My sister and her husband would be co-facilitators, mingling with guests and dancing to all the numbers. Together we would make sure everyone felt welcomed and watered. The "other stuff" wouldn't go away, but we could avoid it just a bit longer.

My last two days with my mother were August 11th and 12th. I remember them, alternatively, like salt that dries on the skin after an ocean swim, or, like fresh water washing away the tightness: soothing and relieving.

When it came time to dress for the party, I put on a pair of pale-pink, stretch leggings I had bought downtown two days previously. I donned a long-sleeved, stretch merino in deep lilac and over the top of that, I pulled on a black, long-sleeved, possum-wool, short tunic. I wasn't dressed for a party, but I hadn't come to NZ with my party gear. I thought I looked OK (but definitely not Parisian).

Mum, once dressed, looked every inch the "La Parisienne."

"Don't you have anything else to wear?" She was clearly critical of my attire.

"I didn't come with my party wardrobe." My sulky retort was reflexive, without thought.

"I'm going to wear the same leggings as yours." Was she gloating or just having some fun teasing me? Or was she doing her "sister act" again?

Regardless, I didn't want to be "hooked," didn't want to engage in bitchy female repartee. I didn't want to feel the sharpness of rivalry between two women. But there it was, where it had always been, where it all starts, where it is all learnt: in the relationship between mother and daughter.

I had a sudden flashback to a time when we had been in Venice together. It must have been forty years ago. I could still hear the excited outrage in her voice when an Italian lad pinched her bum. It wasn't because she had experienced the stereotype of the Italian male as a "truth," that she was thrilled. It was because he had chosen her bum and not mine! There had been four cheeks to choose between and it was one of hers that was the chosen one. She had collected a great tale for her friends at home, but most of all she had felt young enough to be pinchable in Italy. She could pretend to be my sister and not my mother. That is, until I tried to guide her across a busy road. Then she claimed full ascendency. "I'm the mother!"

"F' crying out loud!" I muttered, rolling my eyes and shrugging in true Latin style.

But we weren't in Venice on August 11th, 2022, dressing for her final party in Wanaka, New Zealand.

She walked into the lounge, wearing light grey leggings. They were identical to my pink ones and she had bought them from the same shop the day after me. They looked far better on her than on me. She was much slimmer than me for one thing and grey was a more elegant, Parisian sort of colour than pink.

When I saw her dressed in the same clothes as me, only better, I was miffed.

"Wear what you want!" I threw out in a sullen tone.

It must have been blaringly obvious that she had displeased me because she changed her trousers to a pair of old black faithfuls. She still looked far better-dressed than I did. My mood was a combination of irritation, sulkiness, and guilt, which translated into clipped sentences and pursed lips. I made a point of stating that I was a Kiwi not a Parisian and I didn't care what I looked like. This was so far from the truth that it would have been funny had I not regressed to the age of early adolescence; a time when appearance was a deadly serious affair. It was the age of fresh beauty, lipstick, breasts, and what to wear. It was a time of unconscious rivalry between females for male attention. At that precise moment in time (and at the official age of seventy) I hated my mother with the passion of a fifteen-year-old. It was different from the rage of a five-year-old who didn't want to be told what to do or say, but it came down to the same thing: I was my mother's child and it just wasn't possible to keep the relationship free of uncomfortable feelings. I was clear about one thing though—I did not want to leave Wanaka and my mother the following morning carrying hatred or anger in my heart.

I really did not want that to happen.

LE HAIM!

The celebration of life—my mother's life—was an

unmitigated success. The sun beamed outside the floor-to-ceiling windows, showing the calm waters of the lake with its mountain backdrop. The snow came down to the water's edge at the top of the lake.

Mum's friends poured in, wearing big smiles and their best clothes. They did not come bearing gifts or condolences. They came for a party! When the room was full and buzzing, Maxine gave me the thumbs-up. I leapt, in a manner of speaking, onto a small table, shouted, "Ladies and gentlemen, on your feet please for Tom Jones!" and hit the Play button on the sound system. The speakers blasted Tom, screaming, "I'm Alive!" Maxine and I worked the room, getting anyone who could walk onto their feet (except Martin, who could only stand on one leg). We had everyone punching the air and shouting, "I'm Alive" with each refrain. It was epic! Helen, usually a model of British restraint, grinned and bopped along to Tom. Daphne, not usually given to overt displays of extravagant behaviour, was up and moving it. I loved them for loving my mother enough to celebrate life (in what was surely an unaccustomed manner). They were truly very dear friends.

Mum's next-door neighbour, Steve, got her onto the dance floor and whirled her through the Bee Gees' "Stayin' Alive." Jo's broad-brimmed, red felt hat bobbed and throbbed in the throng to the disco beat.

Jean, used to tough mountain climbs, boogied with the energy level of a mountain goat. "It's a very special occasion, Lynne." Jean winked. "I'm wearing my mascara for her."

"Your mother is a very special person. We've been good neighbours to each other." Donah, from the cottage opposite said. She and Mum shared a Scottish heritage.

Donah spent the afternoon beaming, bopping and sipping. Mum had great neighbours.

Maxine, Craig, and I were the only ones to make speeches. It felt odd to talk about Mum in front of her living presence. It was hard to get the pitch right. It had to be a celebration and not a lament. It wasn't a birthday and it wasn't a funeral. I made the speech Mum wanted me to make. I was professionally gay and personally sad.

Mum took centre stage for group photos. The "girls" lined up for the Tai Chi photo and then the Mahjong "girls" lined up for theirs. They could have all been classmates, posing at an old girls' school reunion. I don't know what everyone talked about because I didn't participate in any conversations. I left my sister to do the socialising. I was DJ, MC, and keeper of the gate. It suited me fine. I guessed that Mum steered all conversation away from her plight and made sure she was the one asking the questions. *It's a good strategy*. I had made a career out of asking questions. *For different reasons, of course*, I told myself.

"People like to talk about themselves and feel someone is interested in them," she had said. I couldn't disagree with her on that one.

It also keeps you safe. Your story remains within your walls.

I had wanted to explain that people asked for coaching when there were cracks in the wall or they had lost their way in the story. I didn't tell her that but I did want to knock down her walls. And, I wanted to keep her safe. I wanted psychological healing for her before she died. And, I didn't want to rock her boat any more than it already was. Any coach worth her salt knew that wanting something for someone else was a sure-fire way to screw up the coaching process, as I was only too aware from trying to manipulate her previously.

The day before the party, Interflora had delivered a wreath from friends in France. It was a perfect adornment for a coffin or a grave.

"Si si c'est pour une amie très chère qui est mourante, effectivement, mais elle veut célébrer sa vie d'abord!" I could see the perplexity on the shop assistant's face registering that she was ordering flowers to be delivered to an elderly lady in an obscure rural town at the bottom of the world—who was still alive, but the flowers were for her funeral. The wreath sat on the hearth in the cottage, until it was placed, along with other flower bouquets, in front of two photo boards set up in the party room. One displayed Mum's early family life and the other showed her at various dos or on exotic holidays overseas. None showed her three children. She was young and beautiful in all of them.

LOVE'S MAGIC, AUGUST 12TH, 2022

The morning after the party Mum was up before anyone else. She was standing in her blue fluffy dressing gown at the kitchen counter. She was fumbling with the liquid morphine, trying to pour the right dose into a small spoon. My sister and husband were still asleep. It was around seven-thirty, before the sun was up.

I watched her, motionless, for a few seconds. Then, without bidding, my heart settled on Love's hearth.

I approached her softly. My arms opened without thought. I took her in my arms, gently.

"I love you, Mum."

"I love you too." The words caught in her throat.

"Thank you for everything. Thank you for making this life here possible. These have been the best ten years of my life. They would not have been possible without you. Here, I was able to become the person I have always wanted to be.

"I will miss you, Mum." I was sure beyond doubt.

"I will miss you too."

We stood there in an embrace that felt real, for the first time. There had been times in the past when we had embraced, but I had always felt self-conscious at such a show of emotion with her.

In the kitchen in Wanaka when we dropped our embrace, I was not embarrassed. I floated, eyes closed, spread-eagled on a warm sea. The freshness of an early-morning tropical sun kissed my eyelids. I basked quietly in this moment of light. I gave thanks for the gift of love and the life I had been given. At the eleventh hour, the words had come of their own accord. I had been able to tell her simply and sincerely that I loved her.

The four of us had breakfast together as if it were any other day. We packed the suitcases into the boot of Craig's car for the return journey north. We took our last photos together in brilliant sunshine on the front lawn. Mum and I walked together past the other cottages to the letterboxes at the entrance. Hers was number four. I took my last photograph of her posing in a sea-green jumper, one hand on her black-and-grey letterbox. She had a multi-striped scarf draped elegantly around her neck. She was wearing sunglasses and her smile was just a little lopsided. I caught sight of her neighbour, Donah, in the background. She was hovering discreetly nearby, knowing about this farewell. She would be Good Samaritan to Mum when Maxine, Craig, and I left her on her own.

I climbed into the front passenger seat of Craig's car. I peered into the rear-vision mirror for one final glimpse of my mother. She had her back to us, walking side by side with her neighbour, back up the way we had just come. I smashed the roof of the car with my fist and let out an ungodly howl of anguish. All the pain of a wounded animal—or a lost child—plastered the inside of the car with its messy yowling and sobbing. Craig put the car in low gear, my sister took my hand, and they both gave space and respect to this unanticipated explosion of grief.

We drove slowly down to the edge of the lake. I stood on its pebbled shore, arms held wide, a gaping wound, vulnerable, before the terrible wellness of the world.

I listened to the silence of water, unbothered by even the slightest breeze. I breathed the cool, crisp, clean air. I watched sun and snow in a dazzling embrace scatter light, like so many sequins across the lake.

Down at the edge of Lake Wanaka, the Great Mother Earth offered me Her comfort and I let Her in.

She gave me Her most perfect day. She held Her breath so nothing would disturb the reflections on the water we drove past. She wore the same colour, deep azure blue, the entire day and at the end of it, She offered a full moon whose light shone on pastures dotted with tiny white sheep. I spent that day in the presence of Her Grace as She shared her exquisite winter beauty. It was as if the sorrow that sought to embed itself in the marrow of my mind was refused entry by Her query, "But how can you be sad when you see Me like this?"

JANUARY 19TH, 2023 - STILL A LONG WAY TO GO

I turn my thoughts away from the last time I journeyed back to Christchurch August 12th, 2022 and focus on the current trip back.

I'm sorry to leave the McKenzie Country and its wide-open tussock lands, but it's an easy cruise over Burkes Pass on State Highway No. 8 and into Fairlie. Geraldine is all but closed when I finally reach its rural outskirts. This is a place where I had liked to stop with Mum for a cup of tea and something fancy to nibble on. But it's no time for a nostalgic stop, with the light fading and another couple of hours of driving still ahead. I pass through Mayfield, Springfield, and Darfield. All traces of the devastation that the earthquakes of 2010–11 wreaked on my hometown have disappeared from Darfield.

Darfield was the epicentre of the first one. Each successive earthquake knocked Christchurch to its knees, toppling houses off the port hills and traumatising the population. My mother had planned to go to the cinema on February 22nd, 2011, but some friends had suggested lunch instead, so she was with them in the centre of town when the earth began its then familiar shake, rattle, and roll. With equal familiarity, the seventy- and eighty-year-old ladies propelled themselves under the dining room table. When the shaking stopped, Mum skedaddled home on foot, through the city centre, past bloodied faces and the city's emblematic symbol: its cathedral, collapsed in a ruin of historical stone. Ross had been on the phone at her place, at the perimeter of the Central Business District, when it happened. The apartment was still standing, a tribute to its solid box-like design, when she finally made it home. She and Ross chucked a few things into his SUV and very slowly made their way through the mess and the snail trail of cars to the other side of town to my sister's place in a northwestern suburb. The trauma inflicted on her and thousands of others that day was the beginning of her move to Wanaka. News broadcasters that day informed the world about the deadly Christchurch earthquake of

February 22nd in which 185 perished, but the Fukushima catastrophe in Japan at the beginning of March quickly claimed the world's media attention—and the people of Christchurch were left in "peace" to wade through liquefaction, clamber over rubble, and bury the dead.

A year later, Mum was living in a cottage in Wanaka, made possible by her son, her two daughters and a lot of help from her daughter-in-law.

CHRISTCHURCH (JANUARY 19TH, 2023)

It's dark by the time I park in Maxine and Craig's driveway. I empty the boot and sort my clothes into piles for packing the day after next. I decide what a first-time, self-published author should wear to her book signing and lay that outfit aside. This time I do want to look a little foreign—a little French—a little Parisian. My mother is not here to give my choice the once-over with her critical eye. I wish I felt happier about that, I miss her. I finally lie down, switch off the light, and find I'm too wired to sleep. My thoughts wander back a month to when I flew into Christchurch.

When I walked into my sister's house on December 24th, 2022, Mum's ashes were sitting inside what looked like an oversized shoebox on a round glass-top table in the conservatory. There was no connection between the mother I had said goodbye to on August 12th and the box on the table. Before leaving Wanaka, Mum had given me a small, crystal, candlestick holder that someone had given her for the same purpose she was, then, asking me to use it for.

"Would you burn a candle for me during my cremation? It's such a lovely idea."

I had no difficulty agreeing to such a beautiful gesture.

After she had left her body and it had been taken to the morgue to await cremation, I wrote to the undertakers to find out the exact time her cremation would begin. I wanted to be certain I would comply with her last wish. It was to be at 9am Tuesday, November 21st, which made it 9pm November 20th, in France.

CREMATION

I invited a few friends who had met Mum to light candles at that time. My friend and a professional singer, Sarada, recorded herself on her phone singing "Amazing Grace." I had faith that the enchanted power of her voice singing the praises of the angels would soothe any soul wandering along a heavenly pathway. I bought a beeswax candle that fitted perfectly into the candlestick holder my mother had given me, placed a white rose on a homemade altar, prepared incense to burn, and selected some texts to read. I chose one of her favourites "The Desiderata" and one of the last poems I read to her over the phone, "My Brilliant Image" by Hafiz. It was to be the little funeral service she didn't want but which I thought she would be happy with: modest but intimate. It was no one else's business! Even though I did tell a few people about it.

At nine in the evening of November 21st, 2022, the makeshift funeral service ran according to improvised plan. Sarada's voice filled the air with haunting melodies. I read. Richard, my husband, spoke. Friends sent photos of themselves and their burning candles. The candle, itself, in its bequeathed crystal holder, took five hours to burn—the amount of time it takes for an adult human body to burn and its ashes to be processed and placed in an urn.

ASHES

On Christmas morning 2022, my sister and I "tackled" the ashes. We wore surgical gloves and scooped the remains of a long and rich life into small plastic bags. We had done the same thing with our father's ashes but I had forgotten how much ash a body produces once it is cremated, and how heavy it is. Standing in the conservatory at Craig and Maxine's house, facing Mum's ashes in a box on the table, we chatted as if we were consulting Mum on where exactly she would like her ashes to be scattered, put, or buried.

"Now, Mum, we know you liked to get around, so here's what we're thinking. We know you said you wanted to be sent off in a wave down at the beach—just like Dad."

"You also told me you fancied resting on the floor of the lake in Wanaka."

"And we think you'd also like to be with your father down in the cemetery in Dunedin."

"It might be really nice to be next to Nana and Aunty Nola in the crematorium gardens here in Christchurch."

"I'll take you back to Paris, so you can be close to that lovely rosebush you planted in our garden."

"I was thinking I'd like to keep you here in our garden, in Christchurch, too."

Mum agreed with all our suggestions, of course.

Our chatter protected us from the atrocity of absence and finitude.

We had been invited by friends of Maxine and Craig to share Christmas lunch with them. We were both grateful that our first Christmas without Mum would not be at home. Their house was a "palace" isolated at the top of Governor's Bay Road, overlooking the whole of the harbour inlet. The first settlers had arrived down there in Lyttelton back in 1850, trudged with all their gear to the top of Port Hills, and looked down on the flat plains of Christchurch on the other side. How extraordinary that first view must have been and how exhausted they must have felt after their six-month journey out from England in a sailing ship. I felt wiped out after the thirty-six-hour plane journey and was glad we hadn't planned on doing any major amounts of walking during the afternoon. It was a warm and sunny Christmas Day. We planned to go down to Brighton Beach at sundown, walk back towards North Beach, and surreptitiously disperse some of Mum's ashes into the to-and-fro of the incoming tide.

But by the time we got there at the end of the day, the wind had turned cold, clouds had gathered in a low sky and the surf was pounding the shore. The beach was devoid of people, so we had no need to disguise our actions. However, we did walk further up the beach, away from the car park. People were huddled inside their cars, watching the thrash and tumble of the waves. I didn't want to be a conspicuous object on the tidal landscape, but most of all, I didn't want a strong nor' easterly wind to blow the ashes back in my face before the sea claimed them. A classic gag was also a real possibility.

LAST DAYS

Mum had finally left Wanaka on September 13th. I had spoken to her just before my sister was due to drive her back up to Christchurch to the Ngaio Marsh Retirement Village.

"Retirement? Not palliative?" I had queried when Maxine had called me to tell me about her choice of places.

"It's got 'options' but they're not splashed all over the brochures. Craig and I think it's perfect for Mum." Maxine had done all the research for a suitable place and had chosen Ngaio Marsh for its appearance, its reputation, and its proximity.

From looking at their website, I understood further reasons for her choice. There was a little stream running through the property. There were flower beds and cut lawns; a central atrium, and separate cottages offering assisted-living conditions. These details were not for Mum—she was past caring about how well the grass was cut. I called her to check, for myself, that she knew what she was doing. The short conversation gouged another hole in my heart.

"Are you sure this is what you want to do?" My voice was soft but firm.

"I need care, Lynne. I can't do it on my own any

more. Having someone pop in to do my dressings on a daily basis is not enough." She was clear, with no sign of hesitation.

"You know that when you leave, you will not come back." There was no time left for pussyfooting.

"Yes, I know."

"Is this the moment, then? Are you sure?" I wanted to be sure.

"Yes, I'm sure."

That was it, then.

Maxine managed the seven-hour motorised ordeal to Christchurch on her own. I admired my sister's strength and practical courage, once again. She was a quirky combination of talented artist and Florence Nightingale. I wondered whether she and I had fallen out of the same cauldron. We couldn't possibly have shared the same genetic mix!

So, Mum moved from a vibrant social life and a house she had made her own, to a hospital bed in a single room with one window. She lay down there and did not get up again, except to go to the bathroom. She got all the care she could possibly wish for, but no one could take away the pain. My sister arranged for visits from monks and priests; a forensic psychiatrist, friends of ours, family: anyone who might relieve the agony and the burden of the dying process for an hour or so.

Our conversations had shortened to brief phrases since she had lain down to die. Those too, were over as they increased the doses of morphine and added fentanyl to the cocktail. Several times Maxine and I both thought that this was "it" but "it" dragged on. I took to reading her poetry whenever my sister called, which was most evenings, my time. I could not think of anything else to offer and had no idea if I was helping or hindering her journey. I remembered the road trip to Makarora when I had thought I was doing something she would enjoy, but she had confessed afterwards just how ill she had felt. Maybe it was the same now. Maybe I was forcing her to make an effort to listen when all she wanted was to be left alone. I hoped, at least, the sound of my voice was a lullaby, even if the words themselves were incomprehensible. Maybe I was reading for the living rather than the dying. I did not know.

Despite the fact that accompanying the dying is an ancient practice, our society has done it's best to ignore its importance. Few people receive or seek training in how to assist a loved one on his or her final journey. Neither my sister nor I were any more au fait than the next person. It was a hit-and-miss affair. I prayed for her release.

My sister, who checked in with her every day, seemed to think that Mum still had "work to do" before she checked out. I imagined she was impatient to die—to get it over and done with, so she could get on with something else. That's how she had been in life. She "got on with it." That could have been her credo. It could be her epitaph. But did she first have to dredge through all the pain buried beneath her bones before she could be released? There was nowhere for her to go, nothing more for her to do, no one she had to be with. She was alone with whatever her morphined mind was throwing up at her.

I imagined, in my mind's heart, the Great Mother's arms wide open, smiling benignly, waiting to receive her. There was no condition attached to Her love. It was so easy in my mind's eye. Why couldn't my mother just let go? Why the agony? But her journey wasn't my journey and I couldn't travel her road for her. Over the phone I spoke to her closed eyes and ragged breathing.

"Take all the time you need, Mum. You will know when it is time to let go. It's your call." Torn between wise old woman and bereft child, I didn't know who I thought I was kidding. Like her, I wanted "it" to be over but didn't want her to leave, either. I wondered how people coped with the fatigue of trying to be present with the dying and awake to the living when the dying went on for a protracted period.

I remembered Sidney Pollack's film, *They Shoot*

Horses, Don't They? I had seen it a long time ago, but scenes from the movie remained with me and returned with great clarity. During the Great Depression, young people take part in a dance marathon. The last couple standing wins a substantial cash prize. Others pay to watch them suffer, collapse, and possibly die. The film had left me despairing of the helplessness of the human condition. I had felt keenly the futility of a human life. My mother's agony seemed to me to be equally cruel and pointless, but no other choice was available by that stage.

New Zealand introduced The End-of-Life Choice Act in 2019 and, following a referendum in 2020, it came into force in November 2021. I had read all the documentation online and had realised that Mum met all the criteria, except the essential: She had to request it herself. We had discussed the issue when it was part of the referendum and she wanted to debate it in her discussion group back in 2020, but by August 2022, the subject was no longer just a debate. I didn't have the heart to raise the question with her again.

By mid-November I could not imagine any purpose for the senseless suffering I was witnessing every evening on a small phone screen. Her form, shrunken, was still adorned in green silk pyjamas. Her features were gaunt, made more so by the absence of dentures. Her breathing was laboured. Assisted dying seemed like an excellent idea and one that I would seriously entertain should I find myself in similar circumstances. *Or would I?* The subject was still in the realm of debate for me, since my death knell hadn't sounded yet. My brother, Ross, had been too positive to have even imagined that he was dying. He and Mum were of a similar ilk, so perhaps Mum was still clinging to a belief that this wasn't really happening.

But it was Englebert Humperdinck who had the last word. Maxine called me at 12h45 on November 19th. Her voice was full of excitement.

"She's gone—she's left—that's it! We were playing 'Please release me, let me go,' and, she was! She left on the refrain!"

Emerald green silk pyjamas and Engelbert! Seriously? My mother didn't stop amazing me, even unto her last breath!

LIFE GOES ON—MAXINE'S ART STUDIO

It's 11am, January 20th 2023. I'm in a spacious room on the first floor of the Arts Centre, across the road from the Christchurch Museum and Botanical Gardens. The Arts Centre was "my" university fifty years ago, before the campus moved to Ilam. Much of this historical building collapsed during the earthquakes, but it's slowly finding its way back to its former stone grandeur. Maxine's walls feel solid and look colorful. I'm here to sign copies of my book today for friends and family.

I've set up "shop" behind a trestle table arranged along one wall. From my seated position, my eyes pick out a small pastel of a waterscape, sitting on an easel on a shelf at eye level. It makes me think of the lake I have left down south in Wanaka. I remember my arrival at the cottage on Boxing Day.

FINAL FAREWELLS

I drove down to Wanaka the day after Christmas. I unlocked the door to the cottage and found it exactly as I remembered it when I left on August 12th 2022.

I thought that the makeshift cremation ceremony in Paris in November had brought closure. I thought releasing her ashes into the ocean on Christmas Day had brought closure. I thought trowelling more of them into the earth beside her mother and sister had brought closure. Nothing, absolutely nothing, prepared me for the tsunami of grief that bowled me over when I stepped back into "Mum's" house late afternoon on December 26th. I was a blubbering kid whose mummy had gone off and left her on her own. She didn't know when her mummy would be back or what she would do if her mummy didn't come back. I was bawling my eyes out like that kid and unloading the car at the same time when Donah popped across the way,

"Good to see you again, how are you?" Big smile. She'd just arrived home and hadn't even unlocked her door yet. Her adult handicapped daughter stood waiting patiently on the doorstep. I fell into Donah's arms, sobbing uncontrollably. I was incomprehensible but she got it immediately. She walked me inside, sat me down, and put the kettle on. She made me "a cuppa": the time-worn British recipe for all ills. She had always been there for my mother and now she was there for me. I didn't know if she specialised in "Saving the Burneys" but I did know a cup of strong black tea did the trick.

"What were you thinking, going into the house on your own for the first time since Maureen left?" she asked with a gentle smile.

"Total naivety," I replied ruefully, when I was able to string two words together again.

She left me to go open up her own cottage and let her own daughter in. Her daughter could see her mother just across the way through the large front window and trusted she would be back. Mine would not be back.

NEW YEAR'S DAY, 2023

A wind blew in off the lake most of the day, but by late afternoon, the waters of the lake were unruffled. It was peak holiday season, but if they were not having a picnic down by the lake, many holiday-makers had already gone home or had wandered into the township for an evening drink and meal.

Jean and I drove down to the lake and parked at its edge. We were already in our bathing suits. We tucked tiny plastic bags each containing a spoonful of Mum's ashes into the front of our suits. I donned plastic shoes to protect my feet from the pebbles that led the way into the water. We waded slowly out into the lake, until the water was at chest height and our feet stood on a sandy bottom. No one else was around. The sun had begun its gradual summer descent. We were out far enough for our feet to bounce lightly off the lake floor and for us to feel the weightless joy that deep water brings to a body. Light patterns, like so many fish nets, danced daintily on the surface of the translucent water. We each released the contents of our packets into the water.

"Mum, it's New Year's Day. There's not a breath of wind. You would love it here right now. You whispered you wanted your ashes to lie at the bottom of the lake. So here we are, Jean and I. Don't worry, no one can see us. We are leaving a part of you here in this lake. Thank you for the poetry of this moment that Jean and I share in your honour. OM Shanti, Shanti, Shanti—Peace, Peace, Peace."

"God bless, Maureen, my dear friend."

We watched, mesmerised, as the ashes sank slowly, in the light, through the water, to find their resting place at the bottom amongst the rock and the sand. They did not disappear in the flurry and crash of an ocean wave; they slid gracefully, elegantly, just as my mother had been, to anonymity and peace.

After a little bit, the chill of being in a mountain-fed lake caught up with me. I began a slow push back to the shore, leaving Jean to commune a while longer with her friend, in the light, on her own.

REVERIE INTERRUPTED

Two Asian girls pull me back from the lake edge and its dying afternoon light to Life's insatiable quest for expression. They wander around my sister's art studio, curious, oblivious to the intensity of my memories. It is unlikely that two young Chinese-speaking girls will buy a book in Christchurch about a pilgrimage in Spain from a writer based in France—but stranger things have been known to happen.

A day later, I am on a plane, once again, heading north to winter. I have Mum's silverware in the hold and a tiny wooden box with a leopard-skin design on the lid containing a few more ashes in my carry-on luggage. I'll store the silverware and feel reluctance to bury the final remains in a garden I will leave one day.

It's a long way home.

Questions

What kind of relationship do you have with your mother, and can you see her as a person as well as a mother?

What do you like about her as a person but not as a mother?

What don't you like about her as a person but like as a mother?

If you had a magic wand, what kind of mother would you conjure up?

In what ways has Mother Nature been a source of comfort in your life?

What are you doing to protect Her from coming to harm?

How do you celebrate the fullness of your life? How often?

PART SIX

Denudare — To Uncover

LIFE'S A SOAP

It's easy to get caught up in a soap. You get hooked on the drama of the everyday lives of a group of people, who fall in and out of love and sometimes do terrible things to each other. There is a soap that plays every night on French TV, after the eight o'clock news and weather forecast and just before primetime. Its catchy theme song is in English and the characters are mostly thin, blonde, and gorgeous. They all live in fabulous apartments and have marvellous jobs. It's set in Montpellier, but it's only because the actors speak French that I believe that. They could be in Florida or somewhere that promises French viewers a touch of the exotic. It's been playing five nights a week since August 2018. Like all good soaps, it's hard not to tune in if the TV is on.

In a recent episode one of the protagonists, a doctor married to a successful businesswoman, is offered a DNA test for his birthday. He discovers he has a daughter and a grandson who show up on his doorstep for the weekend. He tells his best friend, a detective inspector, about it. What the viewer witnesses is his elation. He is giggly and bursting with joy and disbelief. I know exactly how he feels. I know because that is precisely how I felt about my brother from the time I heard about him, to the time I met him, to the time I spent with him in New Zealand and France. What interests me and will keep me tuned in for future episodes is what will happen to him when reality interrupts the fantasy. I don't know what the outcome will be but am certain that the scriptwriter will bring the character of Dr Alain back down to earth with a bit of hard-nosed reality.

It was the same for me. I had put my brother on such a high pedestal from the time I met him that no mortal could have survived the rarified air up there.

He didn't exactly fall off the pedestal so much as let me down. It was such a small event that it hardly seems worth mentioning. I'm not sure what a scriptwriter would do with the episode.

After Ross left the radio industry, he moved to Wanaka and bought a bike business and a travel business. I never really understood what the connection was, but my brother was a businessman, so I guessed he knew what he was doing. He sent me pictures of him cycling in Vietnam on one of his rental bikes, so I imagined that his company sold cycling packages to exotic destinations. I know he already owned the company in 2012 when he came to France for my son's wedding but don't remember which year he bought it. We planned to cycle the Central Otago Rail Trail together on my next trip to New Zealand.

JANUARY 1ST, 2013

Everything was planned. Accommodation along the four-day trail was booked. The bike pickup was arranged. I had my padded cycling shorts and cycling gloves all ready. I was really looking forward to some adventure time with my beloved brother. Even after almost twenty years, I still looked at him the way a young child looks in wonder at a Christmas tree. We were planning to set out from Clyde on January 2nd. An old mate of his was joining us, another Ross. He and his wife were already in Wanaka and were planning on meeting us the following day in Clyde.

We met at Florence's, a local café in a rural setting with an international flavour. Ross and Petrea were there. Maxine, Mum, Craig, and I were all seated around a large table indoors. New Year's Day was on the chilly side that year and all the outdoor tables were full anyway. We ordered coffees, teas, and snacks amidst the hustle and buzz of a packed café.

"Listen, Sis, I'm not going to be able to do the trail with you and Ross." His words hit me like a cattle prod.

"Why not?" My disappointment was blatant. My tone, petulant.

"It's a really busy time of the year for us and I just can't afford to be away for five days. I'm really sorry, Sis."

"Yeah, of course. I really understand." And I did. I knew what it was like to run your own business. I knew summertime was peak season for his bike business. I started wrapping my disappointment up in a conciliatory tone.

"Petrea and I will ride with you both tomorrow as far as Chatto Creek. We'll leave you there and you and Ross can go on without us. We've already notified the three hosts accommodating us along the trail." He's got it all worked out. Of course he has. He's a planner. He's known this for some time, obviously. *Why am I the last to know?* No one else is saying anything. They're just listening and sipping.

"Does Ross know? Is he OK to do the trail with me? We barely know each other." I know my disappointment is falling out of its wrapping. I push it back in again.

"Well, it'll be a great day together tomorrow." I can match him for positive thinking when need be. I know when Mum, Maxine, Craig, and I do a post mortem on the news back at the cottage later, I will defend him (as I know my sister will). We will find reasonable excuses for him. Our mother will be harsher but then, her story is not our story. We will not ask Petrea what is really going on. It still strikes me as uncharacteristic behaviour for my brother. Maybe he and I both have stardust in our eyes when we look at each other. He can do no wrong in my eyes and I, in his.

If anything were amiss, would he tell me? I would tell him because he is my elder brother and fulfils my fantasy of what elder brothers are like. Elder brothers are wise. They are always there for you when you need them. They listen. They give sound advice. You can ask them questions that they always have the answers to. This is codswallop that I love to believe but can't believe because my perfect brother has just let me down.

The following day, as planned, we met up with the other Ross and his wife, who was going to follow the trail in her car and meet us at the end in Middlemarch. It was a perfect day. I looked ridiculous in my biker shorts and helmet but up to the ride to Chatto Creek where we said goodbye to my brother and his wife. Ross, his mate, and I, continued on for a further three days of cycling. We got to know each other quite well. He was a true gentleman: kind, considerate, and talkative. We talked a lot about my brother, but neither of us could truly figure out what made him pull out of the trip that he had planned and put together for us all to enjoy. It was a great trip.

I took great pictures. We stayed in great places with great hosts. It was different without my brother but no less enjoyable. I had no regrets about going ahead with the adventure without him, but I remained puzzled.

A few days after the ride, back in Wanaka, my brother called me. We talked about the trail, but he wasn't really listening.

"Sis," he said over the phone, "I need to get hold of some cash. I was wondering if I could ask you for a loan. I'd be able to pay it back with a sizeable interest rate—better than the bank's." I felt like a porcupine suddenly put on the defensive. I could feel the "quills" on the back of my neck, quivering.

"How much?" I asked and he told me. It was an astronomical sum. I didn't say "yes" and I didn't say "no."

"Can I pop round this afternoon, so we can discuss it, Bro'?"

"Sure, that'd be great." Everything was great.

NO, it wasn't! No one in our family had ever asked me for a loan before. I didn't remember any of my friends ever asking me for a loan. I had never borrowed money from anyone as far as I could remember. The unspoken rule was "If you can't pay for it, you can't have it." But my brother and I hadn't grown up in the same family. His rules were not my rules. He had always seemed to be flush. I wasn't angry with him. I wasn't disappointed in him. But I wasn't tempted to comply with his request, either. I was lucid and resolute. If he had to ask me, it meant he was desperate. Both his kids were planning big, elaborate white weddings just like my son and daughter-in-law. Of course, he couldn't afford to go cycling with his sister and his good mate Ross. That he should ask me for such a large sum of money meant that he was in deep shit and he wasn't telling anyone about it. I had the money in a savings account. I could have let him have it, but intuition told me that this sum might be little more than a drop in the ocean.

I don't know how a scriptwriter would have portrayed what happened that afternoon when I went to see my brother. I don't know whether what was said between us made for good TV viewing. I do know that from then on, I no longer looked at Ross through stardust. I grew up. He was a man of appetites and he was now having to pay for the mismanagement of them. And I loved him no less. He was my brother.

"Bro', I am not going to lend you this money because I don't want money to ever come between us. I love you too much."

"That's OK, Sis. Really. I just thought I'd ask." I see that he is relieved, glad even.

Did I imagine that? I knew I wasn't solving his problem for him, but I didn't know what the problem was, really. I waited for him to share, but he couldn't—or—wouldn't. Things came to a head a year later and both his businesses went for a song. He began the long haul of reinventing himself from scratch in Otematata.

In January 2017, we finally went cycling together. For two days. Just the two of us. This time I was wearing top-notch French sportswear. Freebies from a client. We joined the Alps to Ocean Trail at Lake Pukaki and rode to Lake Ohau for an overnight stay. It was hard work, but I wasn't about to complain. The deep and meaningful never happened over dinner at the lodge, but I do remember him saying somewhere between mouthfuls that he ran other people's businesses far more effectively than he had ever run his own. He was lucid. He wasn't someone who looked backwards, so I never asked if he regretted moving to Wanaka and leaving the Radio Network with its comfortable salary. He was someone who, when he wanted something, put all his energy into getting it. He refused to let money stop him—even to the point of letting other people's money get it for him. He believed so fully in himself that I don't think it ever occurred to him to entertain a doubt. But that was me seeing and hearing him from the outside. If he ever doubted himself, he never shared that with me. The closest I got to a glimpse of the man in full was the small smile he gave me when I refused his request for a loan. I believed, and continued to believe that he, too, was grateful for one less strand of entanglement over money. I never understood his relationship to money. I loved his generosity but failed to see what it was costing him. Perhaps my lack of generosity towards him was a source of disappointment to him. Perhaps I let him down when he needed me. We never had the conversation. I had not factored his dying into my thinking. Once that began, everything else became irrelevant.

And now he's gone. His ashes are buried in the same grave as the parents who raised him and gave him everything. He was my brother. I only loved him.

Questions

Have you ever lent money to a friend or family member? How did it work out?

What place did money play in your family of origin? What place does it play today?

Have you ever been let down by a friend or family member? How did you handle it?

Name two impediments to love.

If you could rewrite the script of your life, what would you still include? Leave out?

Acknowledgments

Book writing is still a novelty to me and I am still learning about how it all comes together, thanks to the support of very specific people—and sometimes, thanks to a conversation with someone, sometime, somewhere.

I am indebted to The Little Writing Group, which has been meeting online every Sunday evening for the past two years. Each Sunday we take turns to read our "stuff" out loud and then receive supportive feedback about what works and what needs reworking. Kris, Rita, Mark, and Philippe, I thank you all so very much. You are all great writers. You all deserve to be in print.

Thank you, once again, to James Nave. Your observations and "nuggets" of wisdom kicked my story in the right direction. Thank you to Christina Thiele, who seems to intuitively understand what will please me in the way of design. Thank you to Jennifer Sanders for unfailing support and encouragement—for taking this whole business in hand and pushing it with dogged determination to become a book that can be sold to others. Thank you to Laurie Gibson for editing it with kindness as well as perspicacity. You engaged with the story, not only as an editor but also in a way I want a reader to engage with it: "This is about me too."

I am also grateful to Helen Burroughs for her meticulous proofreading. Her keen eye caught errors and inconsistencies that would have otherwise slipped through.

Sarada Yadava, old buddy, you know how much I appreciate your contribution.

Many thanks to Marilyn Welsh for accepting to be my first reader. I appreciated your encouragement and I respect you deeply for your kindness and generosity.

Lastly, and most importantly, I offer deep and sincere thanks to members of my family for their willingness to share my vulnerability as I searched for words that would relay my authentic experience of our family while not betraying theirs. It has been quite a task. I hope I honour you and that you feel "safe" reading what has to be my personal perception of events.

About the Author

Lynne Burney was born in Christchurch, New Zealand, in 1952. She has lived and worked in France for more than four decades. She's been an executive coach for over twenty-six years and has run her own school—LKB School of Coaching—in Paris for the past twenty-three years. She has a son and two beautiful granddaughters.

Her first book, *Once a Pilgrim, Always a Coach*, took readers on a pilgrimage to the tomb of Saint James in Santiago, Spain, and was published in 2022. Her second book takes readers on a journey of joy and loss and subsequent grief. Most of all, though, it is a celebration of human resilience. Both books are a toast to life.

Postscriptum

On the evening of March 15th, 2024, I held a "blending of the ashes" ceremony in my garden in Paris, witnessed by Barbara Morgan* and Richard (my husband). Barbara had been my guest for a 3-day family constellations event in the city. Thanks to those people who did their family constellations during the 3 days, it became obvious to me that I had one more movement to make in regard to my mother and brother, that would bring their souls safely home to lie under a rose bush together. I mixed a very small amount of ash from both their bodies on a saucer that had belonged to my Nana, my maternal grandmother. Symbolically, the son was reunited with his mother, the one who gave him life.

Barbara Morgan's website — www.cominghome.org.uk

Printed in Great Britain
by Amazon